Official **Know-It-All** **Guide**™

MONEY MANAGEMENT
FOR COLLEGE STUDENTS

Karin R. O'Callaghan

Fell's

Frederick Fell Publishers, Inc.
2131 Hollywood Blvd., Suite 305, Hollywood, FL 33020
Phone: (954) 925-5242   Fax: (954) 925-5244
Web Site: www.Fellpub.com

Frederick Fell Publishers, Inc.
2131 Hollywood Boulevard, Suite 305
Hollywood, Florida 33020
954-925-5242
e-mail: fellpub@aol.com
Visit our Web site at www.fellpub.com

Published by Frederick Fell Publishers, Inc., 2131 Hollywood, Blvd., Suite 305,
Hollywood, Florida 33020.

This publication is designed to provide accurate and authoritative information in regard to the sub-
ject matter covered. It is sold with the understanding that the Publisher is not engaged in ren-
dering legal, accounting, or other professional service. If legal advice or other assistance is
required, the services of a competent professional person should be sought. *From A Declaration
of Principles jointly adopted by a Committee of the American Bar Association and a Committee of
Publishers.*

Library of Congress Cataloging-in-Publication Data

O'Callaghan, Karin R., 1948-
  Money management for college students / Karin R. O'Callaghan.
     p. cm. -- (Fell's official know-it-all guide)
  ISBN 0-88391-039-X (pbk. : alk. paper)
1. College students--United States--Finance, Personal. I. Title. II.
Series.
  HG179 .O259 2002
  332.024'375--dc21

                                              2002004126

10 9 8 7 6 5 4 3 2 1

Art Director: Elena Solis

Dedication

For my guys Bob, Mike and Brian for their love, patience and support.

———➤•◄———

TABLE OF CONTENTS

INTRODUCTION

1.	Money Makes the World Go 'Round	1
2.	Bank on It	5
3.	Understanding Your Money	27
4.	Credit Cards Are the Chocolate in Your Financial Diet	47
5.	How Much Debt is Too Much Debt?	65
6.	Use Your Money Wisely	83
7.	"Budget" Is Not a Four-letter Word	101
8.	The A-B-Cs of Making Money Work for You	115
9.	The Future is Now	131

GLOSSARY 133

Appendix A Examples of Interest Compounding — 141

Appendix B Time is Money; the Growth of $2,000 — 142

Appendix C Credit Card Payment Examples — 143

Appendix D It Mounts Up! — 145

Appendix E Investment Comparison Worksheet — 146

Notes Page For Worksheet — 147

Appendex F Additional Resources — 148

BIBLIOGRAPHY 149

Acknowledgements

No one can be an expert at everything, but it helps to have lots of knowledgeable friends. This book comes with a lot of input from wonderful people who gave graciously of their time and expertise to answer my questions and ensure the accuracy of my words. I can't thank them enough for their help:

Greg Raetz, CPA, who patiently explained taxes for a lay person.

Larry Mann and Jeff Rose, my legal eagles who kept me out of trouble.

Kim Patterson and Ellen Cooper who helped me with the intricacies of the banking world.

Bethany Ronnberg and Grace McCrowell, two of the best research librarians anywhere. Not only did they help me with research, but they taught me how to speed up my own searches. "If you teach a man to fish you feed him for life."

Most especially, I'd like to mention the thousands of devoted parents who want to help their children, but possibly never had the time or the information to do so. I've been there myself. You were my inspiration. Parenthood is the toughest job in the world and we can't be great at everything, just finding one "great" is an accomplishment.

I really want to thank Don Lessne and Lori Horton who helped this novice through the morass of publishing; they did it with enthusiasm and efficiency.

To all my friends - older and younger - whose brains I picked, mail I borrowed, and memories I taxed, thanks for your patience.

And finally my family who encouraged me, critiqued the book, and helped see it to completion.
THANKS!

Introduction

If you don't know what you don't know, you can't ask the right questions. Consider this, someone sends you a gift; you have no idea it's coming. You don't know that it hasn't arrived because you don't know it was sent. Therefore you can't check with the post office, you can't ask the sender when it was sent or by which carrier, you can't even notify the sender that it hasn't arrived; the sender just thinks you are rude for not responding to the gift.

The same holds true with all phases of life. You have to know the bare facts, basic information, or you can't get to the answers you are seeking. You can't ask a math teacher about algebra if you've never heard the term, you can't ask a banker about float if you've never heard of it, you can't do most things without at least a starting point.

In January 2001, a survey of 1,425 adults commissioned by the Lutheran Brotherhood and Search Institute showed that adults rank "give financial advice" as an "important" action for parents, but less than half "do it". Respondents agreed that these are critical issues, but only 36% said they or someone they knew had actually tutored young people about money.

High schools are too busy teaching the basics and preparing for state certification exams to teach luxury courses like personal finances. Very few colleges provide "life prep" courses that would include this information, although more are starting to present them.

If parents and teachers are not providing the basic financial information, where can young people expect to get it? It's hard to do research on the Internet if you don't have a place to start. You have to know enough to be able to formulate questions before you can utilize the vast resources available via the Net.

That's where this book comes in. *Money Management for college students* is written for those of you in the 16 to 25 age group who may want to learn about money and finance before it is too late. This book is not designed to answer all your questions; it is designed to provide you enough information to start you asking informed questions.

Some of the information in this book you may already know. Some of it you may not need until later in your life. All of it is relevant to your financial life now and in the future. Think of this as a guidebook to your financial well-being.

Through the years divorces have occurred as a result of financial problems. Murders and suicides have occurred because of financial problems. Jobs have been lost because of personal financial problems.

Don't become a statistic. Take a few minutes and learn the basics. When questions occur to you, ask an expert for advice, do research at your library or on the Net, and talk to your friends and parents. Information is the key to stress-free living. You just have to ask the right questions.

Chapter 1

Money Makes the World Go 'Round

If you are like most of us, you never think you have enough money for all your needs. Really, though, it may be that we do not have enough for everything we *want*. **Needs** and **wants** are not necessarily the same thing. Generally speaking, a *need* is something **required for survival:**food, shelter. A *want* is anything else. We often use the terms interchangeably, though; "I need a new dress for the party", "I need a new car", "I need to take a vacation". You *could* go to the party wearing something in the closet; you *could* fix the current car or ride a bus, bicycle, or subway; you *could* vacation right at home with a good book.

According to Webster's, money is "something generally accepted as a medium of exchange, a measure of value, or a means of payment."

In this day and age in the United States, money is a *need*. We cannot acquire the other needs of life without money, cash, moolah, dough; in industrialized countries the barter system went out of favor for general use years ago. It's very difficult to get groceries at the store without some form of money exchanged. You may use cash, checks, credit cards, or debit cards, but some payment is expected at the time of purchase. Unless you grow all your own food, money, in some form, is a requirement of life. Even if you do grow your own food and make all your clothes, money is still a necessity: to buy farm equipment, tools, fuel for the equipment, fabric, thread, and so on.

So let's say it's a given: money is vital to survival. The only thing that varies is how much money is *needed*. I'm not going to begin to define that for you, but by the end of this book you should be able to make logical decisions for yourself.

A HISTORY LESSON

Back in the old days (before even your *great-great*-grandparents were born) people used the barter system. A doctor made a house call and received a chicken, or canned goods, or coal, or a horse-shoeing, or something else in exchange for his service. Goods and services were exchanged for other goods and services. It worked fairly well. Wealth was created by stockpiling goods or by having a unique service to provide.

As early as the 600's B.C., money was invented. First it was coins —gold, silver, copper. The Chinese started using paper currency in the 600's A.D.; it represented certain amounts of coins stored else-where and was easier to carry around. Now instead of giving the doctor a chicken, a patient gave him paper money; today it's lots of paper money and rarely for a house call.

For most people, the way money is acquired is by working. You work for someone; that employer pays you for the work performed. Theoretically, the more you work, or the harder you work, or the better you work, the more money you will receive, either through overtime pay, a raise, or a promotion to a better paying position. In a perfect world, this is how it is supposed to work. Of course, there are employers who do not reward employees appropriately. There are employees who get promoted for "no good reason". There are employees who do not do the work they were hired to do. Life just isn't fair.

Getting back to the monetary system that we enjoy in this country, it's that paycheck that keeps everything going. You get paid; it might be hourly, daily, weekly, biweekly, or monthly. You cash your paycheck. You spend (and hopefully save) the money from your paycheck.

Let's use oatmeal as an example. You buy a box of oatmeal at the ABC grocery. The owner of ABC takes your money and uses it to buy more oatmeal (*stock*) for the grocery; he uses it to buy more equipment for the store; and he/she pays the store's employees.

The money the grocer pays for more stock pays the oatmeal manufacturer who, in turn, pays the box company; the oatmeal manufacturer updates equipment at the oatmeal factory, pays the farmer, and pays the oatmeal company employees. All these employees — at the grocery, on the farm, at the box and oatmeal companies — cash their paychecks and the cycle continues.

Now multiply each purchase by millions and millions. How often do you *just* buy a single box of oatmeal? At least you have to get milk to go with it, maybe some raisins, a little sugar, a bowl to put it in, a spoon to eat it with. Every time a consumer spends money, he or she is helping to keep the system going.

So far we've seen that money is a good thing and vital to the survival of you, your family, your community, and the whole economic system.

In this example, your paycheck (your *income*) is a source of money for you. Your purchases (your *expenses*) are uses of your money. We'll discuss your paycheck in detail in Chapter 3.

When talking about money, we always have to look at the sources and uses of funds; no it doesn't grow on trees or fall from the sky. For an individual (you), there is usually only one legal and reliable source: a paycheck. You may have gambling winnings or an inheritance, but these are not exactly things you can rely on. There are only two recommended ways to increase your available funds: increase your income or decrease your expenses. That's it. Of course, you could turn to a life of crime, but that is neither legal nor reliable and definitely not recommended. We'll discuss investments as another way to increase your income in Chapter 6.

With careful planning (see budgets in Chapter 7) your net paycheck will exceed your needs — food and shelter. Once you have satisfied all your needs, the leftover money is called *discretionary funds* or *disposable income*. That means you get to decide what to do with it. You may go to a movie, pay on a car note, pay college tuition, buy gas for the car, or save it, among thousands of other options. It's your money, you get to decide how to use it. You set your own financial priorities.

Hopefully you will put part of that money into some type of interest-bearing instrument that will provide you with more money (see Chapter 6). This is another way you and your paycheck keep the economic wheels turning: you make deposits at a financial institution. For our purposes we will call it a *bank*, but it could be a savings and loan, a credit union, or a savings bank. These days there is not a lot of difference between them; the primary difference lies in the services they provide and the interest rates available.

Chapter 2

Bank on It

Banks started centuries ago as "money lenders".
Maximilian would loan money to Servicus. In
return, Servi (as he was known to his friends) would
pay Max *interest* for the use of the money.

Imagine asking your best friend to loan you ten dollars for
two weeks. The friend hands you a ten. Two weeks later you
repay the ten dollars to your friend. Perfect. How friendly.
That's what friends do.

However, in a *business* situation, if a business acted this way
they would be out of business very soon. While you have the
borrowed ten dollars, the business *doesn't* have it; that ten dollars
is doing the business no good; they can't buy anything with it,
they can't loan it to someone else, they can't even sit and look
at it. At the end of the two weeks, if you repay just the ten dollars,
the business is worse off than before the money was loaned
because all purchases have been delayed, prices may have gone
up, and they still have just ten dollars.

So money lenders (banks and other companies today) *charge
interest* for your use of their money (*loans*). They also *pay*

interest to you for the use of your money when you deposit it into certain types of bank accounts.

A bank's (remember this refers to any financial institution) *source of funds* is primarily deposits and interest charged. Banks also get money by charging fees for other services they offer.

BANK PROCESSES IN A NUTSHELL

To understand why banks charge some of the fees they do, you have to understand bank operations and the timing of transactions. Most banks are highly computerized. In this day of branch banking they are also very centralized, with one main department possibly overseeing the transactions of numerous branches. For these reasons banks don't work quite the way you might think they do.

When you make a deposit to a bank account (putting money in), the bank records the deposit into the computer and into your account. This money is basically put on hold for a while. There is a record of the deposit, but the money isn't really in your account unless it was a cash deposit. The "while" depends on where the deposit came from.

Example: Your parents send you a check for $500 to cover books for the next semester. You are going to school in Virginia and your parents live in Colorado. Your bank and their bank are not related. You deposit the check at your bank in Virginia. The bank records that you have an additional $500 *almost* available. At the end of the day, actually around 2 p.m. or so[1], the bank collects all the paper transactions of the day (Monday's batch includes any transactions since 2 p.m. Friday) and sends them to a *clearinghouse*. All transactions are sorted by location using the routing

---

[1] The cutoff time varies by bank, so check with yours.

number on each check or deposit slip. (See check sample below.) All in-house transactions are verified and finalized at this time. **The money is officially** *cleared* **and** *posted* **to the appropriate account(s).**

Your Name		Check #
Your Address		Date_____
Pay to		
The Order of_____		$_____
_____		_____Dollars
For_____	_____	
	(Signature)	
:Routing Number : Account Number		Check #

The Federal Reserve Bank acts as a clearinghouse for the member banks in each region. Don't worry, we're not getting into an in-depth discussion of the Federal Reserve yet. Basically all checks are sent to each Fed Branch Bank. The Fed Branch Bank sorts out the data showing Bank A owes Bank B XXXX dollars, Bank C owes Bank A YYYYY dollars, etc. By contacting the other Fed Branch Banks across the country, each branch straightens it all out and gets the right amount of money into each member bank's account. Some of the larger banks have been permitted to act as clearinghouses, but for our purposes we'll use the Fed as our example. The clearinghouse charges each bank a fee for this service.

Each bank is notified of which transactions were completed each night. Assuming your parents have the $500 in their account to cover the check you deposited, those funds are now available to you via your account. If for some reason the funds were not available, the check would be sent back to the local Colorado bank to be handled. This is why it can take several days for funds to become *available.*

See the life cycle of a check below.

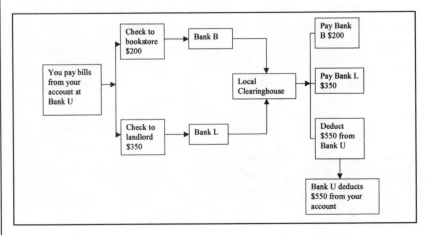

Look around your bank. You will probably see a sign somewhere that says "funds deposited after X p.m. will be handled as the next day's business". In the fine print of your account application there probably will be a disclaimer that "deposits may not be available for two or more days after the date of deposit".

This is called *float*, the length of time between when a check is written/deposited and when the funds are taken out of/or put into the account. On in-house transactions the float is usually very short, about 24 hours. On external transactions (those involving other banks), float can be two to six days.

Example: You have a balance of $50 in your checking account at 6 p.m. on Friday. At 7 p.m. you write a check for $24 for basketball game tickets. On Saturday you write a $17 check at the grocery. Sunday afternoon you write a $200 check to your roommate for your half of the rent. Monday morning you deposit your paycheck of $500; the paycheck is drawn on the same bank as your account.

Technically you were *overdrawn* when you wrote the $200 check, over-

drawn by $191. However, since the earliest any of the checks *probably* will be deposited is Monday morning and they won't post until 2 p.m. at the earliest, you should be okay. The three checks you wrote and the deposit you made will all be treated as Monday's business; it is more likely your deposit will hit your account before the three checks because the paycheck is drawn on the same bank; the checks you wrote may be deposited at other banks. **But don't count on it!**

Generally, if funds are unavailable, they are UNAVAILABLE. That means they don't count as being in your account so don't spend them! Guesstimating when deposits will post or checks clear can be tricky. You should only try to "beat the system" when you are sure you have a deposit **in hand** to cover checks written. This falls into the "Don't count your chickens until they hatch" category. In other words, don't write a check this morning, knowing that the covering check (from your parents) is in today's mail which comes at noon. What if the check doesn't arrive? What if the check arrives on time, but you can't get to the bank to deposit it before the day's cut-off time?

In our example above, change any of the factors and see what a difference it makes. What if the account balance was $300? What if the checks were for $124, $71, and $450, respectively? What if all this occurred on Tuesday, Wednesday, and Thursday instead of over a weekend? What if the paycheck was drawn on a bank across town or from a headquarters out of state?

True Story: A young friend of mine was in the military reserves. Every month he got his paycheck on the second Monday. One weekend, with a balance of $35 in his checking account and knowing he would have the reserve check on Monday morning, he wrote a check for $41.25. The check did not arrive Monday. His account was now overdrawn by $6.25. The bank paid the $41.25 check and charged him $28 for their efforts.

THE FED

"The Fed", alias the Federal Reserve Board, is the central banking authority in the United States. The Board is comprised of the Board of Governors of the twelve Federal Reserve banks. The Fed affects your financial life primarily in two ways: controlling short term interest rates and controlling bank reserve requirements.

The Fed loans money to its member banks so the banks have money to loan to consumers and businesses. The Fed charges those banks interest on the money loaned. The rate charged is passed along to borrowers. When the Fed increases its rates, the banks increase their rates; when the Fed lowers its rates, bank rates get lowered, too. When Fed rates increase, short-term mortgages, car, and other short-term rates also increase. When interest rates increase (or decrease), that means both loan and savings rates increase (or decrease).

When savings and loan rates are higher, savings accounts become more appealing to investors, loans (both personal and business) become less attractive. When people start putting more money into savings accounts, they stop putting their money elsewhere, such as the stock market, real estate, or other investment forms. When businesses stop taking loans because the rates are too high, production may decrease. These actions tend to "slow" the economy. The reverse is also true.

The Fed also controls your monetary life by controlling the reserve amounts of banks. Reserves are the amounts banks must keep on deposit with the Fed to cover outstanding loans and demand accounts. When reserve requirements are high, banks have less money to loan; when reserves are low there is more money available to lend. When there is less money available the cost of it increases, just as in other supply-and-demand situations.

Because of these two functions and their impact on the national economy, people tend to pay close attention to the workings of the Fed.

CHECKING ACCOUNTS

Probably one of the first times you came in contact with a bank was when you opened a checking account. Checking accounts are  known as *demand deposit accounts* because the account holder (you) can demand all the money in the account at any time. The bank has to pay any requests drawn on the account (checks) *on demand.*

Generally, the balance in a checking account is fairly low and fluctuates frequently. Deposits go in, checks get written, money goes out. Most people keep just enough in the account to cover current expenses.

There are all kinds of checking accounts; many banks even provide "special" accounts for students. Some accounts have a limit on the number of checks that may be written in a set time period. Service fees may be charged if the check limit is exceeded. There may be a specific balance minimum that you must maintain in the account.

Some banks pay interest on checking accounts. The interest is usually a minimal amount and is dependent on the balance maintained in the account.

Even in this day of computer banking, checking accounts are still one of the world's greatest conveniences. You don't have to carry around a lot of cash to make purchases and pay bills. Just picture yourself carrying enough cash to buy groceries, buy gas for the car, pay the electric and phone bills, pay the rent, and lots more.

It's so simple: you deposit money into your account at the bank, the bank holds the money, and the bank pays people when they present your check for payment. All you have to do is write a check each time you spend money. Easy, huh?

Well, that's not quite all. You also have to keep track of how much is in your account at all times. If you don't keep up with your deposits and checks-written, you could write a check which will bring your bank balance below zero. When this happens you get an NSF letter from the bank.

NSF

NSF stands for "not sufficient funds". This happens when you *overdraw* the account; spend more than your current balance. Depending on the features of your specific checking account, the bank will do one of three things when presented with a too-large check drawn on your account:

1.The bank will pay the check presented. They will also charge you a fee for having performed this service. Then they will mail you the NSF letter, letting you know that they paid it and that they are deducting the fee from your account. They usually ask you to make a deposit to cover the missing check amount and the fee. Banks may do this if the check is for a relatively small amount and/or if you have made a deposit but it hasn't posted yet (unavailable).

2.The bank will not pay the check; it is returned to the presenter (the person to whom you wrote it). Same routine with the fee and the letter. This is the infamous *bounced check*.

3.The bank will transfer enough money from another account you may have at the bank to cover the overdraft amount. They *may* charge a smaller fee to do this. They will send a letter informing you of the transaction. This type transaction can only be done if you have another account at the bank and if you have "overdraft protection" as a feature on your checking account.

True Story: A college friend of mine wrote a check for $8.00 to the dry cleaners. Unfortunately she had no idea what her account balance was; just assumed there was enough money there to cover $8.00. The check bounced. The dry cleaner waited a day and put the check through again. It still bounced. On the third day, the friend received the letter from the bank informing her of the first NSF and telling her to pay the $16 NSF fee. She immediately made a deposit. Of course the dry cleaners also charged her $40 for the two returned checks - you know those signs posted at service places saying *we charge XX dollars for each returned check?* Then she got the second letter from the bank about the second returned check and the second $16. That $8 check ended up costing her an additional $72. (She did manage to get it reduced to one NSF fee and one returned check fee by sweet-talking the bank and the dry cleaner, but it was still an additional $36.)

```
┌─────────────────────────────────────────────────────────────────┐
│                        OVERDRAFT NOTICE                           │
│ Our records show there were insufficient funds in your account    │
│ 1XXXXXX to cover all of the following items on 10/25/2001         │
│ ITEM DESCRIPTION      ITEM AMOUNT    AVAILABLE BALANCE BEFORE      │
│                                      ITEMS WERE PRESENTED          │
│ CKCARD PURCH          $ 16.50              - $ 15.89              │
│                                                                   │
│ We have paid these items and caused an overdraft on your account, │
│ and a deposit is required as soon as possible. You can obtain     │
│ statement information at most ATM's, or con- tact your financial  │
│ center, Commercial relationship manager, or Private Client Group  │
│ Officer. for further assistance, or for information about         │
│ Overdraft Protection, please call us at 1-800-                    │
│ Please deduct from your account records the insufficient funds    │
│ fee of $29.00 for each item listed.                               │
└─────────────────────────────────────────────────────────────────┘
```

```
┌─────────────────────────────────────────────────────────────────┐
│                        OVERDRAFT NOTICE                           │
│ Our records show there were insufficient funds in your account    │
│ 1XXXXXX to cover all of the following items on 10/09/2001         │
│ ITEM DESCRIPTION      ITEM AMOUNT    AVAILABLE BALANCE BEFORE      │
│                                      ITEMS WERE PRESENTED          │
│ CKCARD PURCH          $ 22.00              - $ 56.50             │
│ CKCARD PURCH          $ 16.75                                      │
│ CKCARD PURCH          $ 15.92                                      │
│ CKCARD PURCH          $ 15.00                                      │
│ We have paid these items and caused an overdraft on your account, │
│ and a deposit is required as soon as possible. You can obtain     │
│ statement information at most ATM's, or contact your financial    │
│ center, Commercial relationship manager, or Private Client Group  │
│ Officer. for further assistance, or for information about         │
│ Overdraft Protection, please call us at 1-800-                    │
│ Please deduct from your account records the insufficient funds    │
│ fee of $29.00 for each item listed.                               │
└─────────────────────────────────────────────────────────────────┘
```

You will notice in the first example above, the difference between being solvent and overdrawn was sixty-one cents. Small change cost this person $29. In the second example, a $29 fee was charged for each item; totalling $145.

The secrets to avoiding NSF situations are (1) an understanding of how banks operate, and (2) keeping a close eye on your account balance. You should always know within a dollar or two what your balance is (see Chapter 3).

In the 70s and 80s, all the talk in the financial world was about the Paperless Society that we were all approaching. Well, we're still approaching it. With automatic deposits, debit cards, automatic deductions, point-of-sale terminals, and computerized bill-paying, we're a lot closer than we were 25 years ago, but we're not there quite yet. Regardless of how it functions, presently a checking account is a convenience we all require; most banks require you to have a checking account before an ATM or debit card is issued.

ATM/DEBIT CARDS

ATM/Debit cards are getting us closer and closer to the paperless society. When used as an **ATM** (automated teller machine) card they allow us to perform banking transactions at hours when the bank is not open; we can get money, make deposits, check balances, transfer funds. When used as a debit card, think of it as a hybrid between a check and a credit card (to be discussed in detail in Chapter 4).

Debit cards have all the convenience of a credit card, just whip it out to pay for things; no presenting identification, no writing, no time.

You had better keep in mind though that debit cards work like a check, only faster. Where you can give a check to the grocery and know it probably won't clear until tonight or maybe even tomorrow, a debit card is immediate. And can be embarrassing. You have to have enough in the account to cover the transaction **right now**, or the clerk or the machine will tell you to try again later (when you have money).

The biggest problem with ATM and debit cards is remembering to enter them into your checkbook register. When you forget, your "known" account balance is WRONG. Big oooops. If you don't want to take the time to enter the deduction into your register right then, just put the receipt into your checkbook and enter it later. Or put it into a pocket; hopefully when you empty your pocket you will be reminded to enter the debit into your checkbook.

When used to get cash, check balances, or perform other banking transactions, ATM cards are a wonderful convenience. But they can be expensive, too. ATM cards are issued by specific banks. Those banks own the ATM machines that they install. If you use one of your bank's machines, most banks don't charge a fee.

To increase the convenience for the customer, the machines are tied into networks. This allows you to use machines virtually anywhere in the world. However, if the machine you use is not owned by your bank, you will be charged a fee to use it. These fees generally start at $1 **per transaction** and go up from there, depending on the bank. U.S. PIRG's (U.S. Public Interest Research Group) 1999 Bank Fee Survey showed ATM fees ranging from 92 cents to $1.50 per transaction; it is safe to assume they have gone up since then at some places. A foreign machine (one not owned by your bank, not necessarily in a foreign country) may not provide all the services of your bank's machines, but at the least you can get cash when you need it.

Caution: Be very careful making cash deposits at an ATM machine. All you have is a paper record of a transaction. If the money doesn't show up when the bank processes the machine, the bank most likely will void the transaction. To get around a cash deposit, give the cash to a friend and have him/her write you a check; then you can deposit the check. Always be sure to write "for deposit only" and your account number on the back of a check when you endorse it.

Because of their convenience, many people use ATM machines like checking accounts: they check balances and get cash frequently. Keep in mind that the balance shown may not be the true balance if checks are also written on the account; some checks may not have cleared yet and therefore are not reflected in the balance shown. If you plan to use the ATM to get "walking around money" (aka cash), try to get a lump sum each week, rather than getting small amounts multiple times a week; this will help reduce your ATM fees.

In early 2001 Dove Consulting (Boston MA) reported that debit card purchases account for 21% of all transactions made each month; credit cards account for 22%; cash is still the most popular from of payment at 39%; and checks are used 18% of the time.

Blocking

There is a little known system used by some retailers to put your money on hold; this is known as *blocking*. When you use a debit (or credit) card to pre-pay for something, that is, to guarantee payment before you know what the balance due is, the retailer can block a specified amount in your account to cover the balance owed. The retailer decides the amount to block. This is used most frequently by gas companies, hotels, and rental car companies.

Imagine that you're going to Notre Dame next month for a big football game (aren't they all at Notre Dame?). You make your hotel reservation, guaranteeing it with your debit card. The hotel has no idea what your final balance will be for the two nights you're going to be there. The hotel puts a block on your checking account for $300 (or whatever amount they choose) to ensure that the money will be there when you check out of the hotel. In the meantime, you could be bouncing checks all over town because that $300 is no longer available in your account. **Moral:**don't prepay large expenses with a debit card unless you are not going to need the money any time soon.

MONEY MARKET ACCOUNTS

Money Market accounts are a special kind of checking account, sort of a cross between a checking account and a savings account. Money market accounts are similar to mutual funds (discussed in Chapter 6) except they invest in short-term securities. With a money market account you usually get a higher interest rate than with a regular checking account. But you are also very limited in the number of transactions you can perform in a banking cycle.

If you exceed the set number of transactions you will receive a letter from the institution letting you know that you made a mistake. Do this often and they will ask you to change to a regular checking account which allows more transactions. The bank will also charge a fee when you exceed the defined number of transactions.

Money market accounts are generally used for saving for specific purposes: college, vacation, whatever. The money goes in, accrues interest, and checks are written only occasionally for those specific purposes.

Money market accounts should be treated as a short-term investment account, rather than as a checking account. The advantages to these accounts are that the funds are more accessible than long-term investments and they usually pay a higher interest rate than a checking account and some savings accounts. Compare money market rates and conditions to other bank instruments before opening an account.

SAVINGS ACCOUNTS

You may have had a savings account as a child. A savings account is considered a *time deposit*; it is expected that you will leave the money in the account for a longer time period than in a demand account.

There are many kinds of savings instruments. Banks *pay* interest on savings accounts, usually more interest than on a demand account. The interest rate varies depending on how long you leave the money (untouched) in the account and how much money there is. The longer the money is in the bank, the greater the interest.

Interest is usually compounded daily and paid on a defined regular basis, monthly or quarterly for examples. That means if you are receiving three percent (3%) annual interest, 3% is divided by 360 days in a year; you get .000083% each day. But since the interest is added to your balance daily, you get interest on the interest if it is *compounded*.

Example[2] :

$100 compounded at 3% for 10 years =		$134.39
$100 at 3% simple interest for 10 years =		$130.00
$1000 compounded at 5% for 10 years =		$1628.89
$1000 at 5% simple interest for 10 years =		$1500.00

Banks like to keep their time deposits high. This source of funds is what banks use (1) to negotiate their loan rates with the Federal Reserve and (2) to make loans.

---

[2] See Appendix A for a larger example of compounded interest rates

Saving money can mount up quickly. If you do it regularly it doesn't even hurt. Start out by saving five dollars a week or a month. We'll go into this more in Chapter 7.

Keep in mind that while savings accounts currently are some of the lowest paying ways to invest, they are also some of the safest. (More in Chapter 6.)

Certificates of Deposit

A Certificate of Deposit is a longer-term savings account. You deposit a prescribed minimum amount (or more) into the account for a defined period of time and you receive a higher interest rate. We'll go into these in more detail in Chapter 6.

LOANS

Banks provide funding for just about anything: college, new house, car, home fix-up, weddings, medical expenses, just "because". Banks acquire money (source of funds) from the interest they charge on loans. Remember, banks are a business and to stay in business they must have income. The interest charged on loans is income for banks. They use that money to pay bills, pay employees, and fund additional loans, among other things.

The rate of interest you pay is based on your ability to repay the loan and the Fed rates charged to the bank. If you have a steady job, a **good credit history**, and/or a recognized ability to repay the loan, the rate charged to you may be less than that charged someone with a less stellar record.

When considering someone for a loan, lenders consider the *loan-to-debt ratio*. The lender's rule of thumb is that a borrower's total debt should not exceed 36% of the annual gross income. That means if your total annual income is $20,000, your total debt (car loan, student loans, credit cards, etc.) should not exceed $7200; a mortgage should not exceed 28% of your total gross income. The problem here is that the bank is dealing with gross income and you are trying to live on net income; we'll talk about this more in Chapter 7.

Put yourself in the bank's situation. Would you rather loan money to someone who is likely to repay it or someone who might spend the money and never repay it?

There is an old adage that *banks only loan money to people who don't need it.* While this is not completely true, there is some truth to it. Most people get loans because they do not have the cash **right now** to pay for something they want or need.

Example: You decide to buy a car after graduation. You have a job all lined up at a reasonable salary. The lender knows that your job will provide you enough money to cover the car note, assuming you're not getting a Mercedes or Lexus. You also have a clean credit report (see Chapter 5), showing you have always made payments on time in the past. You are a good credit risk and the rate the lender quotes you reflects their confidence that they will be paid.

Let's say your twin brother is graduating with you. He has no job prospects and a poor credit history; he failed to pay his credit card bill twice last year and three times the year before. He too is buying a car. The lender may make him a loan, but the rate will probably be higher than the one quoted to you. The lender is not as convinced that Brother is going to pay off the loan, so the lender wants to get as much as possible while the funds are available. Of course if brother *defaults* on the loan entirely (quits paying) the lender gets the car, too. (This is known as *repossession*, or repossessing the car.)

Regardless of the type of loan, the process is the same. When applying for a loan, you fill out forms telling the lender what your income is, what your expenses are, and any other assets you may have. You have to tell them your employment history and anything else which may affect your ability to pay. The bank considers your overall current financial situation and offers you a loan at a specified rate over a specific period of time: for example, a $10,000 loan at 6% interest over five years.

Items Required for a Many Loan Applications
1. W-2 forms for last two years (if available)
2. Information on any other income you want to have considered
3. Employment earnings for the last two years (if available)
4. Last three bank statements for all accounts
5. General value of other assets
6. Complete list of all outstanding debts, account numbers and addresses that you send payments to
7. Social Security Number of anyone who will be co-signing on the loan
   And maybe:
8. Federal tax returns for the last two years

The lender then tells you what your *P&I* payment will be; that's your principal and interest. In this $10,000 example, the monthly note (P&I) will be $216.66.

The important thing to note here is that the loan offer is based on your **current** situation. Only you know what additional expenses you may have coming up: grad school, wedding, baby, new house, new car, new PC. Remember, too, there may be unforeseen expenses, such as medical expenses, travel expenses. What if, six months into your loan, great-aunt Bessie, your favorite relative, dies 1,000 miles away? Of course you will want to go to the funeral.

You can always refuse a loan. Shop around, too; get quotes from different lenders. You are in control of your finances.

Note: When applying for your first loan after college, even with a stellar credit report, you may not be offered the best rate unless you make a down payment or have someone (older) co-sign the loan with you.

Late Fees

Late fees are another source of income for a financial institution (and other businesses). Whenever you have a loan, the payment is due on or before a specific date. If you do not make the payment as required, the bank (or other business) will charge you an additional amount of money as a *late fee*. You can get late fees charged to you by any type business, ranging from your local library, to video stores, to financial institutions. These fees can mount up quickly if you are not careful.

OTHER SERVICES

Banks offer lots and lots of services, most of which have a fee associated with them. Some of the more popular services are:

Safe deposit box - these are secure boxes where a customer can store important papers, jewelry, stock certificates, or other valuables. Boxes come in various sizes and are usually rented on an annual basis.

Investment services - many banks offer investment services ranging from selling government savings bonds to handling stock transactions and trust accounts.

Notary - most banks have a notary public available to provide notary services to their customers. Sometimes there is no fee to the bank's customers, but a fee is charged to non-customers.

Travelers checks - many banks offer the convenience of ordering travelers checks through the bank. There may be a fee associated. Usually the fee is the same as it would be at another vendor; it may be more convenient to get them at your bank.

Check orders - for a fee you can order checks through your bank. Often the fee is more than you would pay ordering checks from an independent source, such as Current Checks, or those other places that advertise in magazines and the Sunday paper.

Cashiers checks/certified checks/money orders - if you need to send a secure check through the mail, or provide one for a legal transaction, the best place to get one is from your own bank. There is a fee.

Stop payments - sometimes a check gets lost in the mail or you change your mind about sending it after you have mailed it. In those instances you can have the bank not pay it when it is presented. You fill out a form and pay a fee and then the bank cannot pay it when the payee sends it in. If the bank mistakenly pays it, they are liable and you get your money back. Stop payments are a good idea when the amount of the check is greater than the amount of the stop payment fee. For example, if you wrote a check for $20 to pay a bill and the check never arrived, it would be worth it to you to put in a stop payment order if the fee is $5, but not if the fee is $20 or more.

Coin counting - if you collect your loose change, your bank may count the coins for you. They may charge a fee. They may only do counting on specific days of the week. If your bank doesn't count coins, then you get to roll the coins into sleeves before the bank will accept them for deposit. Banks usually require that your name and account number be written on each coin wrapper.

Wire transfers - sometimes it is necessary to send money across the country in a short amount of time. When this occurs, a wire transfer is the fastest and safest way to do this. To complete the transaction, you will need the routing number of the bank where the money is going and the name and account number of the recipient. There is a fee.

Overdraft Protection - Overdraft protection is a feature you can get from your bank; you usually have to have more than one account at the bank to get it. This option allows the bank to pay a check when it is presented even if there are not enough funds in your checking account to cover the amount. The bank will either advance the funds from your other account, or pay the amount and bill you for it. You will be charged a fee for this service; the fee may be less than the NSF fee would be, at least it should be no more.

Understanding
Your Money

Many of you may have worked for a regular paycheck at some point in your life. You may have a job while in college. You may not have worked at all up until this time. Regardless, when you graduate you will be making "big money", probably for the first time in your life. When our sons graduated from college, I was amazed at the salary offers they received! You'd better have some self-control with "big" money or it won't hang around very long.

You have to keep in mind, though, when these companies offer you this money, that's a gross amount (no pun intended); that's what they are paying you. It is NOT what will actually appear in your paycheck. For the sake of argument, let's say you start with a job that pays $24,000 a year (it's a nice number easily divisible by 12). That means your gross pay is $2,000 a month. Let's look at the realities.

YOUR PAYCHECK

Paychecks come in all physical sizes, arrangement, and colors. Usually, each paycheck is broken down into sections:

income, deductions, net. Amounts will be shown for the current period (this paycheck) and a cumulative total (year-to-date/ YTD). It may also show any vacation or sick time you have available, depending on the corporate policy. If you are having the pay automatically deposited to your bank account, that account information should be listed.

TIP: If possible, have your paycheck set up for automatic deposit to your bank. This way the money is available in your account even if you are not available to pick up the check at the office.

Income

Your paycheck will probably list the number of hours you worked during this pay period. A pay period can be one week, two weeks, or a month. Most companies pay twice a month; some pay every two weeks; some pay weekly.

Notice that "twice a month" is not the same as "every two weeks", although the annual pay should be close to the same. *Twice a month* generally means you get paid on the fifteenth and the first or last day of the month, or the closest business day preceding those dates. In other words, if the fifteenth falls on a Saturday or Sunday, you get paid the preceding Friday. *Every two weeks* means you get paid **every two weeks**, even if this means you get three paychecks in one month; you will never get less than two paychecks a month. A couple times a year you get a third check in a month because there are five Fridays (or whatever day payday is) in that month.

Note, too, that the *income* reported is your **gross income**, it does not match the amount on the check itself or the amount sent to your bank for automatic deposit. This is also the amount reported to the government for income tax purposes. More about taxes later. If your hiring agreement is that they will pay you $24,000 a year, that amount is computed over twelve months; your gross monthly income is $2,000.

The income section may show *hours worked*. This is very important if you are being paid hourly. Compare the hours reported and the hourly compensation to your records. If they do not match, report it immediately to your supervisor. If you are salaried, the hours worked is not as important because you get paid the same amount whether you work 40 hours or 80 hours a week.

TIP: Always keep copies of your timesheets, whether you are salaried or paid hourly. Keep them for a year. Even if you never have a discrepancy, you can use them to justify asking for a raise.

Keep track of your holiday, vacation, and sick time, too. Don't be short-changed in any category. Likewise, report any lack of deductions; for instance you took a day off and it didn't hit the books. It will eventually be discovered; if you didn't report it your reputation could suffer.

Deductions

Out of every paycheck there will be automatic deductions. These deductions primarily cover various taxes: federal, state, local. The money deducted to cover these is used to pay your taxes at the end of the year. If too much is withheld, you will get a refund, if not enough is withheld, you will owe money. The amount withheld is determined by how many dependents you claim when you file your W-4 and by your gross annual income.

The W-4 is given to you on your first day of employment, probably with a stack of other papers the company Human Resources department will require you to complete. The more dependents you claim, the smaller the deduction from your check.

Some people use this deduction as a type of savings account; they claim very few dependents (you can claim zero), get a lot of money withheld during the year, then get a big refund the next tax season. This is okay if you have no self-control. This is not really a good idea because there is no interest paid on the withholding. You can have the same amount left in your paycheck and then you put it into an interest-bearing account. The account provides the necessary funds to pay your taxes but it accrues interest along the way; thus you have more money than if you had had it *withheld* for taxes.

There also may be deductions for state and local taxes. Same theories apply. At this writing, these taxes are deductible off your federal tax return. You may owe money or get a refund on your state taxes, just like federal. You rarely owe or pay additional on local taxes; often these are just a flat amount; you pay it and you're done.

Form W-4 (2001)

Purpose. Complete Form W-4 so your employer can withhold the correct Federal income tax from your pay. Because your tax situation may change, you may want to refigure your withholding each year.

Exemption from withholding. If you are exempt, complete only lines 1, 2, 3, 4, and 7, and sign the form to validate it. Your exemption for 2001 expires February 18, 2002.

Note: You cannot claim exemption from withholding if (1) your income exceeds $750 and includes more than $250 of unearned income (e.g., interest and dividends) and (2) another person can claim you as a dependent on their tax return.

Basic instructions. If you are not exempt, complete the **Personal Allowances Worksheet** below. The worksheets on page 2 adjust your withholding allowances based on itemized deductions, certain credits, adjustments to

income, or two-earner/two-job situations. Complete all worksheets that apply. They will help you figure the number of withholding allowances you are entitled to claim. **However, you may claim fewer (or zero) allowances.**

Head of household. Generally, you may claim head of household filing status on your tax return only if you are unmarried and pay more than 50% of the costs of keeping up a home for yourself and your dependent(s) or other qualifying individuals. See line E below.

Tax credits. You can take projected tax credits into account in figuring your allowable number of withholding allowances. Credits for child or dependent care expenses and the child tax credit may be claimed using the **Personal Allowances Worksheet** below. See **Pub. 919,** How Do I Adjust My Tax Withholding? for information on converting your other credits into withholding allowances.

Nonwage income. If you have a large amount of nonwage income, such as interest or dividends,

consider making estimated tax payments using **Form 1040-ES,** Estimated Tax for Individuals. Otherwise, you may owe additional tax.

Two earners/two jobs. If you have a working spouse or more than one job, figure the total number of allowances you are entitled to claim on all jobs using worksheets from only one Form W-4. Your withholding usually will be most accurate when all allowances are claimed on the Form W-4 for the highest paying job and zero allowances are claimed on the others.

Check your withholding. After your Form W-4 takes effect, use Pub. 919 to see how the dollar amount you are having withheld compares to your projected total tax for 2001. Get Pub. 919 especially if you used the **Two-Earner/Two-Job Worksheet** on page 2 and your earnings exceed $150,000 (Single) or $200,000 (Married).

Recent name change? If your name on line 1 differs from that shown on your social security card, call 1-800-772-1213 for a new social security card.

Personal Allowances Worksheet (Keep for your records.)

A Enter "1" for **yourself** if no one else can claim you as a dependent . . . . A _____

B Enter "1" if:
- You are single and have only one job; or
- You are married, have only one job, and your spouse does not work; or
- Your wages from a second job or your spouse's wages (or the total of both) are $1,000 or less.

} . . B _____

C Enter "1" for your **spouse.** But, you may choose to enter -0- if you are married and have either a working spouse or more than one job. (Entering -0- may help you avoid having too little tax withheld.) . . . . C _____

D Enter number of **dependents** (other than your spouse or yourself) you will claim on your tax return . . . . . . D _____

E Enter "1" if you will file as **head of household** on your tax return (see conditions under **Head of household** above) . E _____

F Enter "1" if you have at least $1,500 of **child or dependent care expenses** for which you plan to claim a credit . . F _____

(**Note:** Do **not** include child support payments. See **Pub. 503,** Child and Dependent Care Expenses, for details.)

G **Child Tax Credit** (including additional child tax credit):
- If your total income will be between $18,000 and $50,000 ($23,000 and $63,000 if married), enter "1" for each eligible child.
- If your total income will be between $50,000 and $80,000 ($63,000 and $115,000 if married), enter "1" if you have two eligible children, enter "2" if you have three or four eligible children, or enter "3" if you have five or more eligible children. G _____

H Add lines A through G and enter total here. (**Note:** This may be different from the number of exemptions you claim on your tax return.) ▶ H _____

For accuracy, complete all worksheets that apply.
- If you plan to **itemize or claim adjustments to income** and want to reduce your withholding, see the **Deductions and Adjustments Worksheet** on page 2.
- If you are **single,** have **more than one job** and your combined earnings from all jobs exceed $35,000, **or** if you are **married** and have a **working spouse or more than one job** and the combined earnings from all jobs exceed $60,000, see the **Two-Earner/Two-Job Worksheet** on page 2 to avoid having too little tax withheld.
- If **neither** of the above situations applies, **stop here** and enter the number from line H on line 5 of Form W-4 below.

---------------------- **Cut here and give Form W-4 to your employer. Keep the top part for your records.** ----------------------

Form **W-4**	**Employee's Withholding Allowance Certificate**	OMB No. 1545-0010
Department of the Treasury Internal Revenue Service	▶ **For Privacy Act and Paperwork Reduction Act Notice, see page 2.**	**2001**

1 Type or print your first name and middle initial Last name	2 Your social security number

Home address (number and street or rural route)	3 ☐ Single ☐ Married ☐ Married, but withhold at higher Single rate. Note: If married, but legally separated, or spouse is a nonresident alien, check the Single box.
City or town, state, and ZIP code	4 If your last name differs from that on your social security card, check here. You must call 1-800-772-1213 for a new card. ▶ ☐

5	Total number of allowances you are claiming (from line **H** above **or** from the applicable worksheet on page 2)	5	
6	Additional amount, if any, you want withheld from each paycheck	6	$

7 I claim exemption from withholding for 2001, and I certify that I meet **both** of the following conditions for exemption:
- Last year I had a right to a refund of **all** Federal income tax withheld because I had **no** tax liability **and**
- This year I expect a refund of **all** Federal income tax withheld because I expect to have **no** tax liability.

If you meet both conditions, write "Exempt" here . . . . ▶ | 7 | |

Under penalties of perjury, I certify that I am entitled to the number of withholding allowances claimed on this certificate, or I am entitled to claim exempt status.

Employee's signature
(Form is not valid unless you sign it.) ▶   Date ▶

8 Employer's name and address (Employer: Complete lines 8 and 10 only if sending to the IRS.)	9 Office code (optional)	10 Employer identification number

Cat. No. 10220Q

FICA and Other Deductions

Okay, that covers taxes for now. Other required deductions include FICA (Social Security) and Medicare. These are going to help you when you quit working, theoretically. FICA, the Federal Insurance Contributions Act, otherwise known as Social Security, will give you a monthly paycheck once you reach a certain age; the age has a lot of variables so I won't try to define it; at the moment it is over 60. The amount you will receive is based on how long you have worked (it's calculated on the number of quarters worked, four quarters in a year) and how much you paid into the system. Basically it's a retirement fund, but not a very high-paying one.

Medicare will provide medical assistance for you in your old age. You pay the money in now and get medical payments when you are no longer gainfully employed. It's a long-range medical insurance policy.

Virtually everybody pays taxes, Social Security, and Medicare. Consider them involuntary deductions.

Your paycheck also reflects your *voluntary deductions*. You may opt to take the company's health or life insurance program. There may be charitable deductions. You may have an automatic savings plan deduction. Hopefully, the company will have some type of retirement plan to which you can contribute (401K or something else). You may pay the company for a reserved parking space. The list of possible deductions is only limited by your income and your employer's capability to handle the accounting.

Net

Finally, there is an area that reflects what you are actually receiving in this paycheck: the income minus the deductions. The shock could kill you. See the sample check on the next page.

company name and address		
	CHECK NO:	A022087
	CHECK DATE:	01/29/99
	PERIOD ENDING:	01/31/99
	PAY FREQUENCY:	SEMIMONTHLY

mployee name and address	EXEMPTIONS:	FED: 00 STATE: 00	NUMBER:	FED STATUS: SINGLE ST1 STATUS:
	TAX ADJ:	FED: STATE:	STATE CODE:PRI: CO SEC:	ST2 STATUS:
		SSN:	SDI/UC ALT:	LOCAL CODE: LOC1:GV LOC2: LOC3:
			BASE RATE: 2150.00	LOCAL ALT: LOC4: LOC5:

IMPORTANT MESSAGE

HOURS AND EARNINGS					TAXES AND DEDUCTIONS			SPECIAL INFORMATION	
	CURRENT		Y-T-D			CURRENT	Y-T-D		
DESCRIPTION	HOURS/UNITS	EARNINGS	HOURS/UNITS	EARNINGS	DESCRIPTION	AMOUNT	AMOUNT		
REGULAR	86.67	2150.00	173.34	4300.00	SO SEC TAX	133.30	266.60	VAC BALANCE	291.00
					MEDICARE TAX	31.17	62.35		
					FED INC TAX	317.16	634.32		
					PRI-STATE TAX	83.00	166.00		
					PRI-LOCAL TAX		2.00		
					TOTAL TAXES	564.63	1131.27		
					AFTER-TAX DEDUCTIONS				
					PARKING FEE	10.00	20.00		
					FLEXH		133.43-		
TOTAL H/E	86.67	2150.00	173.34	4300.00					
PRE-TAX ITEMS									
401K		430.00-		860.00-					
								CURRENT NET PAY DISTRIBUTION	
								C	500.00
								C	645.37
								CHECK AMOUNT	.00
TOTAL PRE-TAX		430.00-		860.00-					
TOTAL	86.67	1720.00	173.34	3440.00	TOTAL PER DED	10.00	113.43-		
	EARNINGS	PRE-TAX	TAXABLE WAGES	LESS TAXES	LESS DEDS	NET PAY			
CURRENT	2150.00	430.00-	1720.00	564.63	10.00	1145.37			
Y-T-D	4300.00	860.00-	3440.00	1131.27	113.43-	2422.16		TOTAL CURRENT NET PAY	1145.37

Statement Of Earnings ▾ Detach at perforation below and keep for your records. ▾ A Payroll Service By Ceridian

company name and address

461-1

DATE: 01-29-99   CHECK NO: A022087

YOUR ENTIRE NET PAY HAS BEEN DEPOSITED IN YOUR BANK ACCOUNT(S). PLEASE REVIEW
THE "CURRENT NET PAY DISTRIBUTION" SECTION OF YOUR STATEMENT OF EARNINGS FOR DETAILS.

NOT NEGOTIABLE

employee name and address

THE FACE OF THIS DOCUMENT IS COLORED INK ON WHITE PAPER. THE BACK OF THIS DOCUMENT CONTAINS AN ARTIFICIAL WATERMARK. - HOLD AT AN ANGLE TO VIEW

The names have been eliminated to protect the innocent (or guilty). The current (this pay period) gross income was $2150, the deductions were $1004.63, and the net check was $1145.37. Note that this included a 15% 401K contribution, but no insurance deductions (this employee used the spouse's insurance so did not need this company's plan).

If you are receiving a physical check, it should be attached to the pay statement and the amount on the check should match the amount listed as "net income". Likewise if it is an automatic deposit; the statement should show how much was deposited to which account (account numbers have been blanked out in the sample); in most cases you can have the check divided and deposited to more than one account.

Automatic Deposits

Most companies and financial institutions can arrange for your paycheck to be sent directly to the bank. If your company doesn't offer this right away, ask if it is available. All that is required is the routing number and the account number from a check. DO NOT use a deposit slip to input the account number. Some banks have different coding for deposit slips than they do for the actual account number; the check could go to the wrong place; mine did once; it took two months to get it straightened out. Usually you fill out a form and provide a voided check for reference; just take a check and write VOID in big letters across the face of it in dark ink.

BILL PAYING

Okay, so you've got your net paycheck; to be generous, we'll say it's for $700. Remember your gross pay was $2,000 a *month*, that means each biweekly check is for $1,000, before deductions.

Out of this check you have to pay your bills. DON'T PUT IT OFF! Pay your bills as soon as you get your check. Waiting to pay them can result in finance charges and/or late fees or NSF situations. If you get paid on the fifteenth and the end of the month, write out your bill-paying checks the night before each payday. Put the due date in the upper right corner of the envelope, where the stamp goes. Mail the checks to arrive at least one day prior to the due date. After a couple months of doing this you'll know which bills are due when and which ones will come out of each paycheck. For example, if your Texaco bill is due on the 27th of each month, you will need to pay it out of the paycheck you receive on the 15th. If your rent is due on the 1st, it will have to come out of your end-of-month paycheck.

Enter each bill into your checkbook register, under the entry for the paycheck deposit. Subtract all checks. The leftover is what you have to live on until the next paycheck. See sample below.

Sample Checkbook Register

Number	Date	Description of Transaction	Payment/Debit	Deposit/Credit	Balance
D	1/31/01	Paycheck		$700	$750
1102	1/31/01	Texaco	57.32		
1103	1/31/01	Visa	27.00		
1104	1/31/01	Cleaners	8.12		
1105	1/31/01	Church	5.00		652.56
1106	1/31/01	Rent	200.00		
ATM	2/01/01	Cash for movies	20.00		
1107	2/01/01	Grocery	45.83		
debit	2/02/01	Dillards - new jeans	48.56		
ATM	2/02/01	Cash	40.00		298.17
1108	2/03/01	Grocery - party	98.33		
debit	20/3/01	Bookstore- computer disks	12.18		
debit	2/04/01	Lunch at Applebee's	8.65		
debit	2/05/01	Barnes & Noble-Mom's bd	18.35		
1109	2/05/01	Post office- ship to Mom	4.32		
debit	2/04/01	bookstore-card for Mom	3.15		153.19
1110	2/06/01	car insurance pymt	147.00		6.19

Kind of scary isn't it. Be sure to read Chapter 8. It will help you have more money available.

These days many businesses allow you to set up automated bill-paying. This works in one of three ways: automatic checking account withdrawal or a debit or credit card charge. With the automated withdrawal you select from several dates to have the money automatically removed from your account and credited to the billing company's account. With the other methods the company charges the bill amount to your credit card and you pay the credit card when that bill comes due or it hits your debit card like a normal debit card transaction. All methods save you time and postage, but can adversely affect your finances if you forget they are occurring. Also, you must be very careful about giving out your debit and credit card personal information.

BANK RECONCILIATION

Each month you will receive a statement from your bank. This is a report of their records regarding your account(s). Look it over very carefully; bank errors do occur. The statement will show a list of checks which have cleared and posted, deposits which have been recorded, and any fees or automatic transactions. Compare this statement with your records. They should match **exactly**. If they do not, figure out why. Failing to keep your records in sync with the bank can result in NSF situations and/or lost interest.

Reconciling a savings account or money market account is fairly easy because usually there are very few transactions. Compare your records, usually some type of passbook, to the statement. If they do not match, find out what's missing. It's usually a deposit or withdrawal that did not post prior to the statement being printed. Keep your copy of all deposit and withdrawal slips, at least until they have appeared on your statement.

Checking accounts are a little trickier because there is more activity: deposits, checks, debits, ATM transactions, transfers of funds.

TIP: Get a good calculator with a paper tape. They don't cost much and can save a lot of headaches.

Gather your checkbook register(s), your calculator, a colored pen, and a highlighter. Start with the list of checks as reported on the statement. Using the register and the colored pen, mark off each check that is listed on the statement. If a check is not listed on the statement, highlight the box where the checkmark should go in the register. Do the same thing for all other transactions reported on the statement.

On the calculator, enter the current balance showing in the checkbook register. Add or subtract any transactions which did not appear on the bank statement; the ones highlighted. (Add checks not cleared, subtract deposits not posted.) Hopefully this total equals the ending balance on the statement. YEA!!! If you have kept careful records during the month, it should.

Sometimes, however, the balances do not match. RATS! I hate it when that happens. Using the calculator, determine the difference between your register total and the bank total. If the bank ending balance is greater than your register balance, it probably means a check hasn't cleared. If your checkbook balance is greater than the bank's, you probably included a deposit that the bank didn't, or a check was not recorded. If the difference is off by a large amount ($100 or more), it's probably a deposit issue. If it's just a little off ($15.24), it's probably one or more checks.

To find the conflict, (1) recheck the list of checks with your register. Sometimes a check gets a checkmark when it should have been highlighted, or a check clears the bank that didn't get recorded into your checkbook register. Then (2) compare the amounts on the statement to the amounts in the register for each check; sometimes an amount entered into the register does not match the amount entered on the check itself. (3) Verify all automatic transaction amounts; many times it's an ATM/debit transaction that did not get noted in the register.

A last thing to check is (4) the calculator. Recheck your addition and subtraction in the register. I had a calculator once that had stopped recognizing when the 3 was pressed. No transactions that included a 3 were recorded properly. Sure did throw off my bookkeeping!

It may take a while, but you will eventually find the discrepancy. If, after all your research you still haven't found it, take the statement and your register to the bank. Have them find it. It's embarrassing when they do because it's usually something very obvious. A bank may charge a fee to help with this, but it's worth it. Sometimes it is a bank error and usually they are very good about remedying the situation.

TIP: Reconcile your bank statement monthly, as soon as it comes in.

According to the FTC (Federal Trade Commission), if there is a mistake or unauthorized withdrawal using your debit card, you have 60 days from the statement date to notify your financial institution *in writing*. Misuse of your debit card can cost you up to $500 depending on when you report the loss or theft of the card.

TAXES

The old adage is that "the only two things you can't avoid are death and taxes". Scientists are working on the death thing. Taxes are a necessity in our society. Taxes pay for services provided by governments. These services range from keeping up our national parks to national defense to welfare to local libraries to myriad other things.

By the end of January each year all employers and financial entities (banks, stock firms, etc.) are required to file W-2 and 1099 forms (among others) with the IRS (Internal Revenue Service). A copy of each form is provided to the taxpayer. You should get a W-2 for any wages earned, a 1099 for any dividends or interest paid to you or by you (in the case of mortgages or home equity loans).

So once each year we all pay federal income taxes. Most states also have income taxes, but not all of them. That means you pay a portion of your income to the government to help fund all these services. If you have figured your W-4 withholding correctly, the deductions made during the year should cover your taxes; you don't owe any additional and you don't get a refund. It may take a year to determine if your W-4 is correct or not, since presumably you've never had a paycheck this large before. My rule of thumb is, if you owe $100 or less, or get a refund of $100 or less, your withholding is right. If it's more than a couple hundred dollars in either direction, check your withholding for the next year.

When filing your tax returns, there are two types of forms that can be used: itemized and standard. You itemize deductions when you have lots of them and they amount to a lot of money. For most people there is no need to itemize until you have a mortgage and can take off the mortgage interest. The standard deduction is much easier and can be completed by hand if you want; just fill in the blanks for income, take the standard deduction and you're done. Well, it may not be *quite* that easy, especially if you have investment dividends, but it is easier than the itemized form.

TIP: If you want to save the cost of an accountant, and you probably won't need one until you are making *really* serious money, invest in a tax preparation software, such as *TurboTax*. These products help you prepare your tax returns correctly and they offer advice on the next year's tax planning.

Record Keeping

Save your financial records. You may have heard of IRS audits. An *audit* is when a taxpayer's records are selected for review. It can happen to anyone, any year. It may never happen to you. The IRS can review tax returns up to seven years previously; the time period for a normal audit is three years. It's a good idea to keep all your records for seven years. This includes all pay slips, receipts for major purchases and charitable contributions, mileage logs, memos related to income or expenses, medical records, calendars, and investment records.

Keep track of any job-hunting expenses or charitable contributions; they may be deductible.

At our house, at the end of each tax season we put everything into a box: our cancelled checks, bank statements, receipts (medical, charity, and purchases), pay statements, logs, our calendars (both our work day-timers and the kitchen calendar), and copies of our tax returns from that year. We label the box *Tax Year* XX and store it away. We never think about it again. Every few years we throw away the outdated boxes, those from more than seven years ago.

INSURANCES

Insurance is basically a wager with an insurance company; you bet you're going to need funding; they hope you aren't. It's a bet you want to lose because if you win then some major catastrophe has occurred.

Insurance is one area where people think they can save money; it's not a good idea. Most insurance works the same way: the insured (you) pays a monthly/quarterly/annual *premium* (fee) to the insurance company. In the event of a need for the insurance money, the insured pays an annual deductible and the insurance pays the rest. There are millions of variations on how much the deductible is, what the annual cap is, and what the premiums will be.Talk to an insurance expert and get advice from people you trust.

Example: You slip on the ice and break your leg. You don't really think it's broken so you wait to see your regular doctor the next day instead of going to the emergency room. The doctor bills come to $850 (in your dreams!). Your annual health insurance deductible is $200. The insurance pays 80% of the remainder. This means you pay $200 plus $130. The insurance pays $520 (80% of $650). Of course, if you break the other leg later in the same year, you won't have to pay the deductible again, just $170 of the total ($850) because the insurance company will pay 80% of it.

There are basically four kinds of insurance to think about at this point in your life: auto, health, life, and renter's. Once you own a home you will need to consider additional types of insurance. Some insurers offer discounts to students with good grades. Some insurers offer discounts for having multiple types of insurance with the same company.

Auto Insurance

People, especially males, in the under-25 age group pay the highest insurance rates, except for those with poor driving records. But what choice do you have? It is illegal in most areas to drive without car insurance.  If you get caught driving with no insurance, there's usually a heavy fine and your license can be revoked.

If you're in a wreck with no insurance how will you pay for the repairs or a new car?

There are all kinds of options to consider when getting auto insurance: deductible amount, windshield replacement, liability amounts, rental car and towing fees. Consider everything very closely before making a decision and shop around.

Example: In August 2001 a friend, age 23, bought his first brand new car, a Saturn. He shopped all over for car insurance, talking to local agents and researching on the Internet. The first quote he received was $1700 for six months. After much negotiating, he settled on a policy of $1000 for six months. This had a $250 annual deductible with $50,000 in collision coverage and $100,000 in personal liability.

Health Insurance

Hopefully you will be able to get this insurance through your place of employment. The rates will be high, but generally group rates are lower than if you obtain the insurance on your own.

With hospital and medical costs at exorbitant

rates these days, without insurance it only takes one surgery or one serious illness to acquire bills for the rest of your life.

Health insurance comes in all kinds: medical only, medical and dental, hospital only, and so on. There are variations in what is covered, how much is covered, and when things are covered. It takes careful study to be sure you know what you're getting.

There are some items not covered by many health insurance policies; things like dental braces (orthodontia), eyeglasses, orthopedic devices (braces, special shoes, etc.), cosmetic surgery, experimental medical treatments. Don't laugh, "cosmetic" doesn't necessarily mean a tummy-tuck or wrinkle-removing. Lots of things considered "cosmetic" are more for peace of mind than for appearance: could be a "nose-job", post-accident cosmetics, etc. Most of the time you can get coverage for these, but it costs extra. Check with your carrier (insurer) and work out the costs; sometimes it's cheaper to pay directly for the item than to pay for the insurance.

Life Insurance

Again, hopefully this will be provided in some form by your employer. There is term insurance and whole-life insurance. Term insurance is good for limited time periods, such as one year at a time; whole-life continues to grow over time and you may be able to borrow against the accrued total.

At your time of life, you may not be worried about leaving money for your family in the event something happens to you; you may not even have your own family yet! But life insurance is a good idea, if only to cover your death expenses (funeral etc.). Sorry, but it's something you need to think about.

Renter's Insurance

This is the most ignored type of insurance. If you are renting an apartment or a house, you should get renter's insurance. Most young people say, "But I don't have anything worth replacing, so why bother with it?" Let me give you an example.

True Story: I had a friend who went to visit some other friends one hot July Sunday afternoon in Atlanta. They were having a cookout. My friend was wearing shorts, a shirt, underwear, and sandals. A good time was had by all.

My friend returned to his apartment to discover his neighbor had also had a cookout - except it got out of hand and burned down the apartment building. All my friend had left in the world was the clothes he was wearing and the wallet in his pocket; no clothes, no toothbrush, no shampoo, no nothing! And he was supposed to go to work the next morning.

You may not think you have anything worth insuring, but what if you had to replace *everything* you own? It's worth considering.

Now that you are feeling more comfortable with your money, let's throw a wrench into the works. Chapter 4 discusses the greatest obstacle to your financial security: credit cards.

Credit Cards are the Chocolate in Your Financial Diet

Have you ever been on a diet? If not, have you known anyone who has been on a diet? What is the hardest part of a diet? If you answered "avoiding temptation", you're right. When you try to diet, food seems to be everywhere, every time you turn around. And chocolate is the worst of it! Chocolate in the check-out lines at stores, at the movies, on TV, in your friends' hands. No matter how you try to escape it, there it is, tempting you; just one bite, just a little piece, one cupcake won't hurt. "Sometimes you feel like a nut, sometimes..." oh, never mind.

If you give in to the temptation, your diet is affected. Sure, one bite won't hurt, but lots of little bites will sabotage your best plans to diet. Lots of little bites will add weight, just when you're trying to lose it.

Think of credit cards the same way as chocolate: they are easy to find, they are enticing, and once you have put on the weight of a credit card balance, it's next to impossible to lose.

According to a GAO[3] (General Accounting Office) report in June 2001, 3.54 billion credit card applications were mailed in

---

[3] Source: General Accounting Office report GAO-01-773, "College Students and Credit Cards", June 2001

1999. Most teenagers receive their own credit card applications about the same time they start receiving eighteenth birthday cards. These come unsolicited right to the door via the US Postal Service. "Instant credit", "low interest rates", "no annual fee". When you get to college, you are bombarded by offers. Below is a picture of two months' worth of applications mailed to a college student.

Beginner credit cards usually come with a credit limit of $1000, sometimes more. Now who can resist a gift of $1000? It's like free money, right? So you need a new CD or DVD or to furnish your dorm room, with your brand new credit card you can buy anything you want - up to $1000. Cool!

But, wait a minute. Let's think this through logically. Why would anyone *give* you (or anyone else) $1000? There has to be a reason. That reason is "business". Credit card issuers do not give away credit cards out of the goodness of their hearts. They are in business to make a profit. **A credit card is a loan.**

Let's take a minute and discuss the difference between a credit card company and a credit card issuer. The "company" is the big name on the credit card: American Express, Discover, Mastercard, Visa. They provide their name and affiliation to a credit card "issuer": usually a bank. The bank then markets their card(s) to different affiliations (such as an airline or Wal-Mart or a kazillion others) and puts the affiliation's picture or logo on the card. If you have a *United Mileage Plus* card you will notice that the bills get paid to First USA Bank, not to United. The issuer, in this case First USA, is the group that deals directly with the consumer. Got that?

Below are some credit card facts of life, based on applications received by a college-age friend of mine. The sometimes-surprising application terms and conditions can be found later in the chapter under "Selecting a Credit Card".

Credit Card Application Facts of Life

Generally, credit card applications that come in the mail are one of two styles: highly colorful or more professional in appearance. The envelopes they arrive in may have exciting offers, too.

The colorful ones are often the ones touting: **PRE-APPROVED** in bright, bold letters. They may also say the applicant doesn't have to worry about Good Credit/Problem Credit. These are the ones you need to read very thoroughly.

Virtually all credit card applications provide the same basic information: type credit card offered, potential credit line available, and a deadline by which the form must be returned (which usually doesn't mean anything). They may also contain a "reservation number", "solicitation code", or "activation number" that is used by the issuer to identify the applicant. There will also be contact information and instructions for completing the application. And there is a "personal letter" from the company to the applicant extolling the virtues of the applicant and explaining why this "special offer" or "priority notification" is being made. The front or separate page of the offer may also include an "introductory rate" or other rate information, if it is a rate they feel is worth highlighting.

Finally, there is the form for the applicant to complete. This form usually is only a few lines long and may require: applicant's name, address, date of birth, employment status, social security number, current income, name of nearest relative not living with you, and housing status (rent/own). Some forms want your mother's maiden name. They may also ask if you want an additional card; some issuers charge a fee for a second card. Then you sign the form and mail or fax it back.

The critical part of these applications is what is NOT included on the letter/form page. All applications are required by law to define all their fees and policies along with the introductory material. Some do this on the back of the letter; some include a separate paper with this critical data. Regardless of where the information is presented, **READ IT CAREFULLY**; the facts included here may be less stellar than implied with the "greeting" material.

CHARGES

Now if you buy something with your credit card — say a CD for $15.95 — and you pay off the credit card at the end of the month, where is the profit for the credit card issuer? Remember our example in Chapter 2 of loaning $10 to a friend? How do credit card companies make their money? One way they make money is by charging a fee to each retailer that accepts that brand of card.

Another way is by charging the card user. Okay, using the CD as our example, you purchase the CD, charge it on your credit card, and pay the bill in full when it arrives. That means you write a check to the card issuer for $15.95. Where did that $15.95 come from? Out of your available cash, whether it's from an allowance or a paycheck. You now have $15.95 less to spend during the *next* month. So the next month you charge something else; it's soooo easy to do, the card is "everywhere you want to be". Then you charge something else, and something else. At the end of the second month your credit card bill could be as high as $200, or more. You can't pay it in full so you only pay a part of it, say $20. It should be noted here that $20 is more than the normal minimum payment required for a $200 balance (most credit cards carry a 2% or $10, whichever is greater, minimum payment). You now have an outstanding balance of $180.

Gotcha! From this point forward, until the $200 is paid in full, the credit card issuer will charge you interest on that balance. This is where the issuer makes a lot of its money: on the interest charged to the card user. And if you are late making a payment, they will also charge a late fee. Both interest (called *finance charges*) and late fees get added to your outstanding balance. Pretty soon you are paying finance charges on finance charges. A credit card balance works the same as any loan, you pay interest and late fees just as you would on a car loan.

Remember back in Chapter 3 we were discussing your paycheck and we took the view that your net pay, after all deductions would be $700 per paycheck (hopefully). Out of that you will take housing/rent, groceries, utilities (gas, electricity, phones, water). Depending on where you live and your life style, these items alone could run as much as $700 a month (or more); you are now down to $700 a month for everything else in your life. Sound like a lot? You still have to pay for insurances, gifts, entertainment (movies, dates), gas for the car, car repairs, maybe a car note, maybe a student loan, maybe a laundromat or dry cleaner. Now add in a credit card payment. The GAO reported that, on average, college students charged $127 a month to credit cards in 2000. As a proportion of what you have left out of your remaining $700, suddenly that credit card payment is looking like a lot of money. See Chapter 8 for money-saving ideas.

Credit card interest can be as high as 24% annually. Did you know that if you only pay the minimum balance on a 10%-interest credit card each month it could take you over ten years to pay off $1,000? And that's if you don't put any additional charges on the card while you're paying off the $1,000. At 16% interest, it can take over 35 years to pay off a $5000 debt if only the 2% minimum is paid each month. At 18% interest it will take 46 years to pay off the same $5000. What other plans do you have for 46 years from now? Don't believe me? See Appendix C for examples of credit card debt payoff amounts.

But this is the tricky part of the whole thing. The credit card issuers know you will continue to add charges to the card. Hey! You've got to live, right? Because you do not have the cash you are paying on the credit card each month ($20), you use the credit card to maintain your lifestyle —movies, dates, clothes, furnishings for the dorm/apartment. The balance continues to grow while your minimum-payment-due increases more slowly.

The minimum payment is usually 2% of the balance due. If the interest rate is 18% annually (very common), that means you are being charged about 1.5% monthly. Do the math: you pay 2%, they charge you 1.5%; you're only reducing the outstanding balance by about half a percent each month, or less. And that's only IF no more charges are added to the balance. Also, as the balance owed decreases, so does the amount of the minimum payment; that's why it takes so long to pay off a relatively small debt. Think about this the next time you charge a box of chocolate-covered donuts.

If you are being conscientious and making your payments on time, just to show what good sports they are, the credit card issuer will raise your credit limit! That means you can build even more debt.

Look at the actual credit card statement on page 54. At the top of the form you see the balance due ($3,155.88), the payment due date, and the minimum payment amount ($218.88). Under the issuer's name (First USA) you see the Previous Balance ($1467.38), the last payment ($200, more than the previous minimum due [$29.35]), the current purchases ($1881.20) and the current finance charges ($7.21). Looking a little to the right, you see the cardholder's Total Credit Line ($3,000) and Available Credit ($0).

Comparing the credit line to the new balance, we see that this statement indicates the cardholder has exceeded the credit limit.

That explains the large Minimum Payment Due. The $218.88 includes the $155.88 payment to bring the account back into line with the credit limit plus the 2% minimum payment of $63.

The large middle section of this statement details each transaction that makes up the over $1800 in new charges...in one month. Notice there is also an over-the-limit fee of $29 and Finance Charge of $3.19, computed on the previous balance of $1467.38 minus the $200 payment.

The bottom of the statement explains how the finance charges were computed.

This shows one company's statement. While the style and display will vary from issuer to issuer, the same basic information is included on all credit card statements.

This is not intended to be a bashing of credit cards nor of the issuers, because the credit cards are no more at fault in creating a debt problem than chocolate is in creating a weight problem. Credit cards are a wonderful blessing as well as a strong temptation. They're convenient to use; you don't have to dig out your driver's license to use one. They give you good records of expenditures. They are extremely handy in an emergency — like when you have a dead car battery in the middle of nowhere. You can't order anything on-line without one. They're easy to get.

But they must be used responsibly. Credit card issuers are aware that young adults often do not have the maturity nor the strength to avoid the temptations provided by ready cash in the pocket. Recently issuers have changed the tone of their advertising, stressing responsible use along with the convenience.

New Balance	Payment Due Date	Past Due Amount	Minimum Payment	**FIRST USA.**
$3,155.88	01/29/02	$0.00	$218.88	

Amount Enclosed	$.	Make your check payable to First USA Bank, N.A. New address or e-mail? Print on back.

FIRST USA BANK, NA
P.O. BOX 15153
WILMINGTON DE 19886-5153

1131749

⑆5000160 28⑆ 224 2564 19 26 129⑈

FIRST USA.

210-1
645-0

Statement Date:	12/06/01 - 01/04/02
Payment Due Date:	01/29/02

CUSTOMER SERVICE
(in U.S.) 888-399-2586
(call collect outside U.S.)
1-302-594-8200
(en Espanol)
1-888-446-3308
(TDD) 1-800-955-8060

VISA ACCOUNT SUMMARY

Account Number:

Previous Balance	$1,467.38	Minimum Payment Due	$218.88	
(-) Payments, Credits	$200.00	Total Credit Line	$3,000	
(+) Purchases, Cash, Debits	$1,881.29	Available Credit	$0	
(+) Finance Charges	$7.21	Cash Access Line	$600	
(=) New Balance	$3,155.88	Available for Cash	$0.00	

ACCOUNT INQUIRIES
P.O. Box 8650
Wilmington, DE 19899-8650

PAYMENT ADDRESS
P.O. Box 15153
Wilmington, DE 19886-5153

VISIT US AT:
www.firstusa.com

TRANSACTIONS

Trans Date	Reference Number	Merchant Name or Transaction Description	Credit	Debit
12/05	2439900ALSA96DFTB	KMART 00043992 SILVER SPRING MD		$25.17
12/05	2439900ALSA96DFTK	KMART 00043992 SILVER SPRING MD		$10.48
12/05	2466100AL3G44FMYX	BO'S MONGOLIAN BBQ BETHESDA MD		$64.21
12/06	2439900ANSA96DHA1	KMART 00043992 SILVER SPRING MD		$43.37
12/07	2430103APND3WWNKB	WMATA CAT#926 WASHINGTON DC		$20.00
12/08	2416405APRBGHD25J	EXXONMOBIL18 01080944 ROCKVILL MD		$19.95
12/08	2438775AP231WPBKF	BRICKSKELLER WASHINGTON DC		$91.57
12/09	2445501AP3X7K2WNN	DENNY'S #1715 GAITHERSBURG MD		$17.29
12/09	2461043AP2324N90S	GIANT FOOD INC #189 SILVER SPRING MD		$15.85
12/10	2415259AT6G2HP779	AT&T Wireless Services 800-888-7600 NJ		$160.00
12/11	2424651AT8B4YPPAE	KNOT SHOP #7017 WASHINGTON DC		$42.30
12/14	2445501AW3XMZLT84	SUNOCO CLARKS SUMMI PA		$9.60
12/14	2469216AX002F7PT8N	TEXACO INC 91002181169 THURMONT MD		$14.65
12/16	2445501AY3XVYS13Q	SUNOCO WEST HAZLETO PA		$17.11
12/16	2461043AY231YR0S3	DENNY'S RESTAURANT CORTLA CORTLAND NY		$17.52
12/17	2412151AZ00QXN0KT	BLACKHAWK INDUSTRIES 757-4363101 VA		$72.95
12/17	2413829B0BA9DD88H	BORDERS BOOKS & MUSIC 10 KENSINGTON MD		$72.39
12/17	2415813B0S662Z9S2	NORTHGATE CLEANERS SILVER SPRING MD		$15.00
12/17	2430103AZND3XDK2L	WMATA CAT#926 WASHINGTON DC		$20.00
12/17	2444500B0BAB0X1PY	KAY JEWELERS #1180 KENSINGTON MD		$149.45
12/17	2444573B0BAAVPQ53	BLOOMINGDALE'S WH KENSINGTON MD		$103.95
12/18	2461043B02324KLVM	GIANT FOOD INC #189 SILVER SPRING MD		$28.59
12/19	2410838B2615KR1VG	TORTILLA COAST WASHINGTON DC		$29.84
12/19	2430103B2ND3XJ680	WMATA CAT#926 WASHINGTON DC		$20.00
12/23	7441711B50142MJ00	PAYMENT - THANK YOU	$200.00	
12/20	2464000B8A6TATD3M	1667-3 CHECK TO ROBERT		$408.00
12/31	2464000OJA67SA536	1668-3 CHECK TO CHASE AUTO		$363.05
01/04		OVERLIMIT FEE		$29.00
01/04		*FINANCE CHARGE*		$3.19

AN OVERLIMIT FEE WAS ASSESSED WHEN YOUR ACCOUNT BALANCE
EXCEEDED THE ESTABLISHED CREDIT LIMIT ON 01/02/02.

FINANCE CHARGES

PERIODIC RATE(S) AND APR(S) MAY VARY

Category	Daily Periodic Rate 30 days in cycle	Corresponding APR	Average Daily Balance	FINANCE CHARGES
Purchases	.04929%	17.99%	$251.79	$3.73
Cash advances	.04929%	17.99%	$0.00	$0.00
Promotional purchases	.02737%	9.99 %	$356.27	$2.92
Promotional purchases	.02737%	9.99 %	$68.03	$0.56
Total finance charges				$7.21

Effective Annual Percentage Rate (APR): 12.97%

Grace Period Type: A *(Please see back of statement for the Grace Period explanation.)*

The Corresponding APR is the rate of interest you pay when you carry a balance on purchases or cash advances.
The Effective APR represents your total finance charges - including transaction fees such as cash advance and balance transfer fees - expressed as a percentage.

According to the GAO study, at least two-thirds of all college students have at least one credit card in their own name; as many as 13% have four or more credit cards. The average credit card debt of undergraduate students applying for student loans was $2,748. Half of recent college grads left school owing an average of $19,400 on student loans alone.

Of those students carrying a credit card balance (not paying it in full each month), the average balance is $500 or more. If you repeatedly fail to pay your balance in full each month, you may be affected for life. If you think getting more than one credit card is the solution, imagine making multiple $20 credit card payments each month; what does that do to your available cash?

The GAO study reports that in Spring, 2000 there were 5.4 million full-time undergrad students in the U.S.; a salesman's dream. Because the impact of credit cards is so long-lasting, many colleges have started regulating — and in some cases, banning — issuers on campus.

When you are making credit card payments you will not have cash for other things; your choice will be to deny yourself something, or add charges to the credit card balance. If you are a reasonably responsible person, you will worry about paying these bills. The worry will cause stress.

Again, the GAO study found that "...universities cited financial concerns as possible reasons why college students decided to leave prior to graduation." As you get older you may have a family or a home, credit card bills may affect your ability to provide for them. More stress.

Worse still, if you have had several late payments, or no payments, this will affect your credit rating. A poor credit report means you may have trouble getting qualified for a car loan, renting an apartment, or even getting a job. Later on it can mean problems in getting a mortgage for a house. See Chapter 5.

CASH ADVANCES

One of the many conveniences of a credit card is that you can get a cash advance from just about anywhere. You go to an ATM machine or a bank, present your card and they give you the requested amount of cash. The amount gets added to your credit card balance.

The problem is that cash advances are usually charged a different, and higher, finance charge rate than purchases or balance transfers. Be sure you know what you're doing before you do it.

TRANSFERRING BALANCES FROM CARD TO CARD

Many people think the solution to credit card problems is to keep getting new cards and transferring the balance from one card to another. The reason people think this is because the issuers make their offers sound so attractive, "2.9% interest" or some such. Of course 2.9% is a lot better than 18%. But you have to read the very fine print where it usually states that this offer is for a limited time and then the rate changes to something else - definitely something higher than 2.9!

If you only have one card with a big balance it might be worth it to transfer the balance to a card with a lower interest rate, hoping that you can pay it off before the rate changes. Otherwise, odds are, you will be back in the same situation with the new card, or it might be a worse situation.

Sometimes the new rate will be based on a general financial indicator, such as the "prime rate". The Prime, as it is known in financial circles, is the rate the major lending institutions charge to their best customers for loans. Some credit cards — and other types of loans - list the APR (annual percentage rate) as "prime plus XX%", where the XX is some number. This means they will tack an additional percentage (XX) onto whatever the prime rate is at that point in time. If the Prime is 4.7% and they are going to add 8%, your new APR will be 12.7%.

Transferring several card balances to one card with a much lower interest rate is a form of bill consolidation. This can be a good thing IF you close out the original cards and IF the new card's rate after the rate change will still be lower than the original multiple card rates.

Watch out for "transfer fees". This is usually a percentage of the amount transferred. For example, if you transfer $1,000 from another card, the new card may charge you 4% ($40) as a transaction fee. It works like a finance charge and is added to your account balance.

SELECTING A CREDIT CARD

Having said all this, I strongly recommend that everyone have ONE major credit card and forget the rest. Currently there are three levels of credit cards: basic, gold, platinum. The basic card can buy you all the things a "metal" one can, just maybe not as many. The big difference in the cards is in the credit limit — you can get a

Important Credit Card Disclosures

On a separate page or on the back of the application paperwork, all issuers are required to provide information about their rates, fees, and policies. Usually there is a table of rates and fees followed by detailed explanations in very fine print. Examples of possible information are:

Application Fee or Fee for Availability of Credit

    Examples: <u>Acceptance Fee:</u> $100.00 per card (one-time fee)

                  <u>Processing Fee:</u> $25.00 for one/$50.00 for both (one-time fee)

                  <u>Monthly Participation Fee:</u> $5.00 per card ($60.00 annual fee)

                  <u>Additional Card Fee:</u> $15.00 per card annually

Annual Fee or Annual Membership Fee

    Examples: $50

                  waived for the first year, $59 per year after that

Annual Percentage Rate for Purchases

    Examples: 20.9% for average daily balances of $1,000 or less, 18.9% for average daily balances over $1,000

                  15.99%

                  A fixed introductory rate of 0.0% through your January 2002 billing period. Beginning with your February 2002 billing period, a fixed rate of 14.9% daily periodic rate

Grace Period for repayment of the balance for purchases

    Examples: None

                  You will have a minimum of 25 days without a finance charge on new purchases if the New Balance is paid in full each month by the payment due date.

Minimum Finance Charge

    Examples: For each billing period that your account is subject to a finance charge, a minimum total FINANCE CHARGE of $0.50 will be charged.

Other Fees/APRs

    Examples: <u>Cash Advance Fee:</u> 3% of amount of the cash advance, but not less than $5.00.

                  Greater of $2.00 or 3% of the amount of the advance. A fixed rate of 14.9% daily periodic rate

        <u>Late payment fee:</u> $29

                  $25 each time the payment is late

        <u>Over the Credit Limit:</u> $25 each month the balance exceeds the credit limit

        <u>Balance Transfer:</u> $0

                  Same as for purchases

        <u>Penalty:</u> a variable rate based on the conditions explained below

Method of Computing Balance for Purchases

    Example: Average daily balance including new purchases

Other Items

    Examples: <u>Return Item Charge:</u> $25.00

                  <u>Auto Draft Charges:</u> $5.00 per draft

                  <u>Copying Fee:</u> $3.00 per item

higher limit with one of the "metal" ones. But if you don't need a higher limit, and realistically who does?, don't pay an extra fee to get one. Read the application VERY carefully. On the opposite page is a list of the terms and conditions that may appear on an application you receive along with representative wording that may be included. Any or all of these items may appear on an application.

When selecting a card issuer, there are five things to look at:

❖ The card fee. This is usually an annual fee for the use of the card. Lots of issuers offer cards with no fees. Fees for "metal" (gold or platinum) cards may be higher than the fees for a basic card. It may be called a membership fee. Notice on the list above there are fees called "acceptance fees", "processing fees", a "monthly participation fee", and a fee for an additional card (like for your spouse). I have seen one application that included all of these, to a total amount of $240 for one year.

❖ The finance charge rate. How much will you be charged annually if you maintain an outstanding balance? It may be listed as the APR (annual percentage rate). Often there is also a minimum finance charge; this is the least amount you will be charged for an outstanding balance. The minimum typically runs $.50. That means if the finance charge on your account amounts to $.27 one month, you will be charged the minimum amount ($.50) rather than the computed amount ($.27).

❖ The grace period. This is the number of days from the date of purchase that you have without a finance charge, *if your monthly balance is paid in full each month.* That means if you paid your January bill in full and made a purchase of $25 on your credit card on February 3, there would be no finance charge on the $25 until the next month (March). If you pay the February bill in full, there will be no finance charge at all on this $25. However, if you did not pay January in full, the $25 is added to the outstanding balance and the finance charge can be applied to the total from the date of purchase.

❖ The minimum due. If you maintain an outstanding balance, what is the minimum you will have to pay each month? This is usually a percentage of the balance, typically 2%. Once your minimum due reaches $10 or less, the minimum payment amount usually stays at $10; it is unlikely a minimum will ever be less than $10. Remember, however, things like an over-the-limit amount can boost the minimum due.

❖ Benefits of one card over another. Some cards offer rebates, some offer frequent- flyer or frequent-stayer points, some offer various travel options. If you are not going to use the benefits, don't pay for them. Keep in mind with a 1% rebate, you would have to spend $1,000 on your credit card to receive a $10 rebate. To get one free domestic airline ticket, you might have to spend $25,000 or more; is the card's annual fee worth it?

Inasmuch as you will probably receive credit card applications on a regular basis, you may as well comparison shop. Get yourself the best deal. If you find a better deal later, cut up the first card and notify the issuer *in writing* that you have done so; then go with the second. Don't pay more than one application fee a year, though, and don't have more than one major credit card at a time. A good web site to check is **www.bankrate.com**; they provide credit card rate comparisons free of charge.

The important thing in selecting a credit card is to read the application very carefully. There is a lot of fine print. Although many companies offer a "fixed rate", in the fine print it may state that the rate can change with fifteen days notice to the cardholder.

Try to limit your use of other credit cards, too, such as gasoline companies and department stores. Very often you can get a discount by opening a department store credit account. That's fine, do it. Just cut up the card after you get the discount and notify the store *in writing*! The more cards you carry around, the greater the chance that you will find a use for them. Have you ever tried to carry a Snickers™ bar around with you and *not* eat it?

Keep in mind that each credit card application will be detailed on your credit report. See the next chapter for more on this.

CREDIT CARD SECURITY/IDENTITY THEFT

I learned the hard way that there is no real way to keep your credit card secure. If you ever give out the number, whether over the phone, on the Internet, or in person, there is a chance someone will take that number and run.

The best you can do is try to limit your card use in situations where the number might be compromised and **review your statement carefully each month**. If you find some unknown charges or

incorrect amounts on your statement, report it to the issuer immediately *in writing*.

True Story: Some business associates and I checked into a hotel in
California in October for two days. In January, when I received my
December bill, there were over $8000 in charges at stores in
California, charges made in December, long after we had left the state
and returned home, with our credit cards in our wallets. It turned out
one of my travelling companions had the same occurrence. We reported it to the issuer immediately and the charges were negated.

It was determined an employee of the hotel was part of a network,
working several stores in the area. The hotel employee took the credit card numbers from the hotel register and went to the stores to make
purchases; their accomplices at the stores rang up the charges using
just the number, no card. I never heard anything more from the
issuer.

GETTING OUT FROM UNDER CREDIT CARD DEBT

If the day dawns that you decide your credit card debt is too
much, there are several things you can do:

1. List all your credit card debts, the total due, their minimum
payments, and their finance charge rates. Get a handle on your true
situation.

2. Apply any extra money (such as a bonus, an inheritance, a
raise, lottery winnings, or just money leftover from last month) to
the highest finance charge balance each month. For example, if

you increase your monthly payment on a $5000 balance at 24% from $100 to $125, that loan will be paid off in seven years and seven months instead of 25 years.

3. Work on a cash basis only. That means you don't use your credit card for *anything* (with the possible exception of a *true* EMERGENCY).

4. Make fixed payments each month, even though your minimum payment due will go down over time. In other words, if the beginning minimum balance due is $20 and you can afford $25, pay $25 and continue to pay $25 even when the minimum due is $10.

5. Make one time large payments to quickly reduce the balances. If you have a savings account earning 5% and a credit card balance requiring 18%, you can pick up a quick 13% by emptying the savings account and paying off the credit card. Do not touch your Emergency funds, though (see Chapter 7).

6. Call your credit card company and ask for a lower rate. Often they will work with you because they'd rather get some money from you than no money. If they will not negotiate, transfer your account balance to a lower rate credit card and close the first account *in writing*.

Summary

The easiest way to control your credit card charges is to treat the credit card like a debit card. Each time you charge something, enter that amount into your checkbook register. At least you will have a current record of how big the credit card debt is and that should give you pause before you make any further expenditures.

The moral is not "don't get a credit card". That's like telling a dieter to never eat chocolate again. The moral is: "IF you get a credit card, use it responsibly." Just like a diet, it's okay to eat chocolate (or run up more charges) in moderation, you just can't overdo it. Too much chocolate will get your weight out of control; too much debt can get your life out of control. Don't put on more credit card weight than you can lose easily, with the minimum amount of deprivation.

How Much Debt is Too Much Debt?

S
o far we've looked at banks and their different types of accounts, money and its uses, your money, and credit cards. We've seen how easily money can be spent. You should have an idea that it's easier to spend it than it is to get it. If you're paid $20 an hour, you'd have to work 20 hours (2 ½ days) to earn $400. Your net pay for that 20 hours might be $350. You can spend that much on one month's rent or a car note.

In early 2001, the average American household spent over 14% of its disposable income paying off debts[4]. Here's the problem, if your wants and needs exceed your **net** income, you can find yourself in serious debt very quickly. It is especially easy to do when you are first starting out in a new job, new town, new marriage, or new house. It is normal to want everything to be "perfect". You want to furnish the new residence, or make a good impression at the new job, or shower the new spouse with gifts (like a toaster).

The most convenient and fastest way to get what you want is to buy *on time*, meaning you don't have to pay the full

---

amount all at once. Using a credit card or a bank loan are the two most common ways to buy on time. Unfortunately, as we saw in Chapter 4, it is the very ease of credit card use that creates part of the problem. Let's say you buy a new sofa, then you get a lamp, and a bed, and a TV. The total comes to $1100, all put on your credit card. You now have a new monthly minimum payment due of $22. What will that do to your cash for the month? What are you going to cut out of your spending to meet that payment? Fewer groceries? Cheaper gas for the car? No dates? (Note that bank loans usually carry lower interest rates than credit cards, but may be harder to get.)

What if the next month you are in a car accident, not even your fault? You are without a car while it's being repaired so you get a rental; that has to go on the credit card. You have to pay immediately for the car repair, before the insurance check arrives; you have a $200 deductible anyway; the repair goes on the credit card. And so it goes. Unexpected situations are the most common cause of serious debt.

It takes only one major unexpected expense to send the best-laid financial plans to the trash. The trick is the **unexpected** part. You can't predict car accidents, storms, medical emergencies, a death in the family, or the neighbor at your apartment getting his barbecue grill too hot and burning the place down. It is a fact of life that emergencies create sudden and often outrageous additional expenses. You can plan for them, but you can't predict when they will occur.

The biggest problem with too much debt — other than the social and economic ones—

is the missed opportunities. You can't afford to go cross-country to your parents' twenty-fifth anniversary party because of your debts. You miss a favorite uncle's funeral. You pass up a job promotion because it requires a move to a much more expensive locale. The anniversary is a planned event; the funeral isn't; the promotion may be a surprise, too. If you didn't have so much existing debt you could save up for the trip to the party. The sudden funeral and promotion are lost causes because you don't have the opportunity to save for them.

Now that you have seen how easy it can be to acquire a major debt load, let's talk about the problems with this. There are two major problems aside from the one where you just don't have any money to spend, your entire paycheck is being used just to keep creditors off your back. The two problems are in your credit report and in bankruptcy.

TIP: DEBT IS A FUNCTION OF YOUR EXPENSES, NOT OF YOUR INCOME.

If you learn only one thing from this book, that's it.

CREDIT REPORT

A credit report is a record of a borrower's credit history. There are three major companies (Equifax, Experian, and Transunion) that track a borrower's loan performance; how often payments were missed or late; how much was borrowed; overall financial history; any collections processed; even how often credit applications were filed. Every one who has ever taken out a loan (car, student, mortgage) or gotten a credit card of any kind has a credit history.

From that credit history, creditors compare your information to the credit history of similar other people and assign a "score". The higher the score, the more likely the person will repay a loan. It's sort of like SAT scores for finances.

The credit history reflects how much debt you have had and how reliable you were in paying it off. As long as you make regular, on-time payments on your loans (remember a credit card is a loan), your credit record should be in good shape.

Each time you apply for a loan, your credit history is checked. That means that the lender contacts one (or more) of the tracking companies and asks for a credit report. The credit report helps the lender decide if you are a good risk for a(nother) loan. What they really want to know is "are you likely to be able to repay the loan?" In this day of computer speed, the credit check takes only a few minutes.

If you have a good credit history, you will probably get the loan for which you are applying. If you have a bad history, the lender has several options:

❖ Grant the loan applied for
❖ Refuse to grant the loan
❖ Grant the loan at a higher interest rate to cover themselves in case you fail to pay at some point

The greater your total debt burden, the more likely it is that you will be late with one or more payments, or even have to skip a payment at some point. When these things happen on a continuing basis, your credit report becomes less and less favorable. Credit agencies will give you a poor *credit rating*. It will be difficult to obtain additional credit. What if another emergency occurs? How will you be able to pay for the next big expense?

Did you know that, according to the FTC , "Employers often use a credit report when they hire and evaluate employees for promotions, reassignment, or retention?"[5] The employer must have your permission to access your credit report.

Once you have a poor credit history it usually takes at least two years of stellar credit performance before a lender will consider you for a new loan.

The interesting thing is that you need some debt to prove you can handle it; then you can get more loans. If you live on a cash basis all your life, lenders may think that's strange, and since you have no credit history, you could be classed as a bad risk. Weird, I know, but true.

Did you know that the majority of auto insurance companies use credit scoring to help determine the rate to charge a client? It seems insurers believe credit responsibility can be related to driving responsibly.

If you are ever denied credit, insurance, employment, or a promotion because of your credit report, the company denying you must inform you of the reason for their rejection. You then must be allowed the opportunity to "set the record straight".

To correct an error in your credit report, the disputed information must be detailed in writing to the Credit Reporting Agency (CRA). Include copies (not originals) of any supporting documentation you have. The CRA will then reinvestigate the issue(s) and make corrections to your report as needed. It's a good idea to ask them to send the corrected report to anyone who has received a copy of your credit report in the last six months.

---

[5] Source: FTC Consumer Alert, "Negative Credit Can SQUEEZE a Job search", September 1999

BANKRUPTCY

Bankruptcy is a solution to too much debt. In the 90s, people thought it was a quick fix to their out-of-control spending. Run up a lot of debt, file for bankruptcy, debts wiped out, start over. Unfortunately for those who had legitimate debt problems and not just a lack of self control, there were so many bankruptcy filings in the 90s that the laws regarding who could file and when have been changed by Congress and are awaiting President Bush's signature (at this writing). Bankruptcy is no longer as easy a way out as it was in the 90s; and it wasn't the easy solution people thought it was even then.

Basically, there are two types of bankruptcy available to individuals: Chapter 13 and Chapter 7. Under Chapter 13 you may keep a mortgaged house or car and you pay off your debts in regular installments over three to five years. To qualify for Chapter 13 the debtor must have regular income and cannot have excessive debt. When you file for Chapter 13, it becomes public record. How would you like your friends, neighbors, and coworkers to know that about you? How about potential employers?

Chapter 7 is the more severe type of bankruptcy and requires you to surrender all assets that are not exempt in your state. Exempt items are things like household furnishings and work-related tools. All non-exempt items are then sold and the proceeds are used to pay the creditors. Remaining debts used to be eliminated. As of 2001, if the Congressional revision is

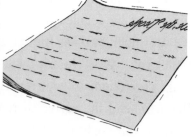

signed, it will be harder to eliminate credit card debt. Chapter 7 probably will appear as public record.

Under the federal Fair Credit Reporting Act, a bankruptcy can remain as part of your credit report for up to ten years. This ten year entry on your credit report is the biggest issue. For that length of time the stigma of irresponsibility remains. In some states credit reports may be checked as a requirement for employment. A recorded bankruptcy will undoubtedly make it more difficult to get a mortgage or other types of credit in the future.

According to the American Bankruptcy Institute, in 1980 consumer (as opposed to business) bankruptcy filings accounted for 86.81% of all filings. At the end of 2000, that percentage had risen to 97.17%. In mid-2001 bankruptcy filings were on track to exceed the 1998 record of 1.4 million filings.[6]

According to the GAO report, people in the 25-34 age group accounted for 29% of bankruptcy filings in 1999. Where did those debt totals that prompted the bankruptcy filings come from? It is unlikely they acquired them over night.

HOW MUCH IS TOO MUCH?

Now that you're sitting there saying "it won't happen to me", let's look at how much debt is really too much. My rule of thumb is, if you or your significant other can't sleep at night because you're worrying about how you're going to pay all your bills, you have too much debt.

---

[6] Source: America Bankruptcy Institute, "New Bankruptcy Filings Break Quarterly Record", August 24, 2001

What if

❖ You owe a total of $1,000 on two credit cards at 20% interest. The monthly minimum payment total is $20. Your monthly net income is $1200. Is this too much debt?

❖ What if you owe $8,000 on one credit card at 18% interest? The monthly minimum is $160. Is this too much debt?

❖ How about if you have to make $400 in minimum payments on $20,000 in student loans and credit cards. Is this too much?

Only you can decide how much debt is too much for your situation. You have to look at the **total debt** amount in relation to your other monthly expenses (housing, groceries) and your net monthly income.

Key indicators that you have too much debt are that (1) you have no savings and no fun, and (2) all your money is going to pay off existing debts and buy groceries. You can't "save for a rainy day" because it's always a hurricane. You fight about money with your significant other. Your job performance is slipping because you are stressed about money and/or not sleeping. Your health is poor because of the stress.

Here are some other guidelines to help you decide:

❖ Do you worry about how you are going to pay the bills?

❖ Do you live paycheck to paycheck?

❖ Are you unable to put money into savings **every month**?

❖ Do you use one credit card to pay off others?

❖ Do you consistently use a credit card for necessities, like groceries and medicine?

❖ Have you gotten calls or letters from credit services about your financial situation?

❖ Do you spend time at work worrying about your financial situation?

❖ Have you had to decline participation in a retirement program at work (like a 401K) because you have no extra funds to invest?

❖ Do you have balances on multiple credit cards?

❖ Do you pay just the "minimum due" on credit cards each month?

You can get books from the library which define percentages of debt to income, not counting a mortgage. I have found that most of them are unrealistic when dealing with the real world. Go with your gut; if you are worried about your debt load, it's probably too much.

FINANCIAL AID

While we're on the topic of debt, let's talk a minute about financial aid. College costs — tuition, books, housing, personal expenses — continue to rise at an ever-increasing pace. In many families the cost of a college education is the second highest expense in the family budget; right behind the mortgage. "In the 1999-2000 school year, the percentages of undergraduates receiving federal aid ranged from 21% at public 2-year institutions to 80% at private for-profit institutions".[7]

Most financial aid is distributed based on need. Sometimes families are not eligible for aid with one student in college, but may be eligible with more than one.

According to the College Board, the 2000-2001 average **annual** student expenses for tuition and fees only, ranged from $3,510 at 4-year public institutions to $16,332 at 4-year private institutions.[8] The College Board estimates that there was over $68 billion in aid available in the 1999-2000 school year; of that amount, about 70% was federal aid[9].

Hundreds of books and web sites are available explaining the types of aid, how to get it, and where to apply. Let's look briefly at the three major types of aid available: scholarships, grants, and loans.

---

[7] National Center for Educational Statistics, January 19, 2002; www.nces.ed.gov/index.html

[8] SOURCE: "'Table 6. Average student expenses, 2000-2001. *The College Board College Cost & Financial Aid Handbook 2002* (2001):33. Copyright ©2001 by College Entrance Examination Board. Reprinted with permission. All rights reserved. www.collegeboard.com."

[9] SOURCE:"'Figure 1. Estimated student aid by source for academic year 1999-2000 (current dollars in billions). '*The College Board College Cost & Financial Aid Handbook 2002* (2001):19. Copyright ©2001 by College Entrance Examination Board. Reprinted with permission. All rights reserved. www.collegeboard.com."

Scholarships and Grants

Scholarships and Grants are the best type of financial aid because they are like gifts; you don't have to pay the money back. The income may be taxable, however. Scholarships are available for just about any type of outstanding, recognized performance: academic, athletic, talent, community service, just because you're a neat person, etc. They are available from colleges, civic organizations, individuals, and just about any other person or group you can think of. Scholarships are available to first-time students and upper-level students. Usually, scholarship awards are not based on income, neither yours nor your parents.

Generally, scholarships are awarded for a specific amount of money and/or for a specific time period: $1,000 or "full tuition and books for one year" (or four years). They may be tied to a specific school or they may just be a general payment to be used where you want. Scholarships may be renewable. Scholarships may have conditions attached such as "must maintain a B average or better". You need to check the wording of each award. You may accept more than one scholarship at a time.

Grants are the other type of "gift". There are usually fewer of them available. Grants may be renewable by reapplication. Generally, grants are awarded to the best candidate and not tied to income or need.

Loans

Loans are the most common method of financing a college education. They are available from financial institutions, colleges, and governments. Often students cannot get aid from banks or colleges because their  parents make too much money to be eligible, or the student has too little income to be a good risk, or because the interest rates are prohibitive.

Federal student loans, in some amount, are available to just about anyone who applies. The nice thing about federal loans is that the interest rates are very low — at the time of this writing, they are taken out in the student's name, and repayment does not start until six months or more after the student leaves school. The interest on the loan may be deductible. According to Tim Golden, Financial Aid Director for Virginia Military Institute, "It just takes one application to apply for the majority of loans. Once the application has been completed, it gets easier each year." The web site for Federal Aid is **www.fafsa.ed.gov.**

Federal loans are offered for a year at a time and *the student must reapply each year.*The loan provider determines the amount to be paid and the interest rate to be charged. Records are kept and a cumulative total of the outstanding loan amount is maintained. Loans are available to incoming students, upperclassmen, and graduate students. There are specific forms that must be completed. Application should be made several months before the start of each school year or semester. If starting school other than at the regular start time (Fall) — maybe in summer school or spring semester — partial-year loans are available.

Financial aid information and forms are available from high school guidance offices, college financial aid offices, books, the Internet, and private financial institutions. There are lots of opportunities out there and all it takes to apply is some time to complete applications. College financial aid directors are in agreement that one of the greatest drawbacks to aid is that either the students (or their parents) do not read the information completely and make incorrect assumptions about what is going to happen later, or they do not ask enough questions before taking on the debt commitment.

Student Loans

If you have to have debt, student loans are a good kind of debt, because the rates are so low. Student loans, especially those from the federal government, have made college more available for many students. They are usually offered at reasonable interest rates (as low as 5.39% in 2001) and you don't start repaying the loans until six months after graduation. This six months allows the student time to get a job and get settled before taking on a new financial burden. Many students are graduating with up to $20,000 in student loans and credit card debt. As reported in September 2001[10], the default rate on student loans in 1999 was 5.6%; the national consumer delinquency debt rate in mid-2001 was 3.54% on non-mortgage loans[11].

If your student loans total $10,000 at 7% interest and you have five years to pay them off, starting six months after graduation, that means you will be expected to pay about $224 each month until the loan is paid in full.

[10] Department of Education News, September 19, 2001, "Accountability for Results Works: College Loan Default Rates Continue to Decline"

[11] Federal Reserve Statistical Release, "Charge-Off and Delinquency Rates on Loans and Leases at Commercial Banks", September, 2001

It would be a very good idea if you started to put money aside to repay these loans while you are still in college. Even if you only save a little bit while you are in school, you will be that much ahead when the loans come due.

The National Association of Colleges and Employers (NACE) reported that "the graduating class of 2001 has had to work harder than its recent predecessors to get jobs, but ...we continue to see many new grads getting substantial starting salary offers."[12] You get to define "substantial" for you. Some representative *average* salary offers were:

English majors:	$31,501
Sociology majors:	$28,812
Business admin:	$38,449
Electrical engineering:	$51,910

Once you land that high-paying job, start taking the loan payment amount out of every paycheck you receive, starting with the first one. If you get in the habit of spending your entire check, when the loans come due it will be much harder to cut back on your expenses.

A Word of Caution

Keep a close eye on your debts while in college. If you have too many when you graduate, the situation may limit your job selection options. You may not have the luxury of being able to wait for "the perfect job" offer because you need income right away to pay creditors, pay the deposit on an apartment, or move across the country.

[12]NACE Press release, July 11, 2001, "New Salary Report Shows Many New College Graduates Continue to Command Top Dollar"

GETTING OUT FROM UNDER

Have you noticed all the commercials for "easy credit", debt consolidation loans, and home equity loans? There must be a reason for them. Have you noticed the mood change in credit card commercials? They now talk about using credit cards "responsibly". Some credit card bills even include "cardmember tips" that help the card-holder use the card more intelligently. Debt in this country has gotten out of hand, and it is starting to be noticed.

1. Once you have serious debt, the quickest solution is to stop spending. I didn't say the easiest, just the quickest. Don't buy anything that is not a true **NEED**. Groceries are a need, movies are not. Even some groceries are not **needs**: ice cream, popcorn, cookies, as examples. Look on it as a chance to lose some weight while reducing your debt load.

2. Each year, order a copy of your credit report from one of the companies, or get a combined report. Review it for any errors. Get the errors corrected as soon as possible. Instructions for correcting errors are usually included with the report.

3. If you don't have a budget, read Chapter 7 and get one *immediately*.

4. If you have debts, pay off the ones charging the most interest first. For example, you owe $2000 on one credit card charging 20% interest and $3000 on another card at 12% interest. Pay the minimum on the second card each month and as much as you can over the minimum on the first card each month.

5. Do the math and determine if debt consolidation will help you. If you move both balances to a third card charging 2.9%

interest for six months will that help you pay off the balances sooner? Remember, at a lower interest rate, the balance owed grows more slowly. Be careful of this solution, though. Check to see what the finance charge will be at the end of the introductory period.

6. Close unneeded credit card accounts. Write the issuer, ask them to close the account, and ask that the credit bureaus report that the account was "closed by the customer."

7. Pay all bills on time. This enhances your credit rating and decreases your late fees.

8. If you are saving on a regular basis, stop until your high interest debts are eliminated IF the debt interest rate is greater than the savings interest rate. For example, if you are paying 18% on credit cards and "making" 4% on a savings account, it makes more sense to pay off the credit card.

9. Talk to non-profit organizations like Consumer Credit Counseling Service; they have helped thousands of people get their finances under control. They are available in most major cities. Check out the Internet for other sources of help.

10. Can you get another job to increase your income? Be careful with this one, though. It sounds practical, but transportation, clothing, or child care expenses may eat up the extra income.

11. Pay the highest possible consistent amount on credit card debts. That means if the monthly minimum is $20 and you can afford to pay $30, pay $30 every month, even after the minimum has dropped to $18, $16, or less.

12. The best solution is to never get in this situation in the first place. That's why this book is telling you the facts of financial life while there is still time. Talk to your parents, ask them their solutions for financial stability.

Sources of Credit Reports

Equifax	1-800-685-1111	www.equifax.com
Experian	1-888-397-3742	www.experian.com
Transunion	1-800-888-4213	www.transunion.com
For a combined report		www.truelink.com
		www.getoutofdebt.org

Other sources are available on the Internet.

Use Your Money Wisely

Because you are smart and because you are reading this book, we will assume that you are open to new ideas. We also assume that there will come a time in your life when you will have some residual cash, money that is not needed for rent, food, entertainment, or other "necessities" of life. By using your smarts and reading Chapter 7, that time can come fairly soon. So what will you do with your leftover money?

For starters, let's not think of it as leftover. You should always carefully plan what to do with your available funds, not just let it vaporize like an alien being. You should set priorities in all phases of your life. This chapter discusses goal setting and investing. We are going to make a further assumption: you are mature enough to start thinking about long range planning.

GOAL SETTING

"A goal is a dream written down." I have no idea who said that, but it's true. If you have dreams, they become more of a reality if you see them in writing. At this stage of your life your dreams are probably very self-centered; that's not "self-centered" as in egotistical, just self-oriented because at this point you are the only one you have to think about. Most people in your age group are not married or the sole support of an aging parent or younger siblings; there are some who are, but most aren't. This is possibly the time of your life when you are the most free to do what YOU want to do, without regard for an impact on others.

It's also a good time, though, to give a passing thought to the future. Some day you may want to marry, or buy a house, or go to grad school, or take a long trip, or have children, or retire at 40, or ... who knows what other dreams you may have? You may not have given your future a lot of concrete thought up to now. The thing is, while you have no other responsibilities, now is the time to start planning financially for the future, because now is when you will have the most cash available. Once you have a family or a house or grad school loans, the expenses start piling up and your discretionary funds are quickly and dramatically reduced.

So where do you start planning for a not-so-distant future? Get out that trusty paper and pen again or use your PC and write down your dreams. Take a trip around the world at 25. Marry at 30 (you don't even have to have anyone in mind right now). Have a two-story house and three kids. Be president of your own company by 28. Get into med/law/grad school. Buy a farm and retire at 50. Buy a brand new car next year. Get a state-of-the-art computer. Own a bed and breakfast. It doesn't matter to anyone but you what your dreams are, just write them down. Now you have goals.

Now take a wild guess at how much each goal will cost. In many cases it will be no more than a wild guess, but do it anyway.

Grad school: $10,000 a year. Trip: $15,000 (depending on whether you're camping or going first class). House: $150,000. Car: depends on whether we're talking Porsche or Saturn. And so on. Talk about a wake up call!

This list should give you the impetus you need to start saving money. Setting goals gives you something to strive for. It's like taking a trip — you can't get *there* unless you know where *there* is. Imagine getting in your car and driving and driving and driving with no destination. You'd just keep going and never stop because you have no final end-point. However, if you're driving to San Diego, you'll know when to turn off the engine.

You're young and carefree with few responsibilities. I'm not trying to burst your bubble, just trying to get you to plan ahead. I have a young friend (27) who is single and financially stress-free. He has a varied stock portfolio worth over $70,000 that he has built since he graduated from college six years ago. No, he didn't win the lottery; he just planned for his future. I have another friend who spends every penny he gets because, as he says, "I'm young. I want to have fun."

Unfortunately, this latter attitude is all too prevalent. That's why bankruptcies were so plentiful in the 90s. The "Me Generation" spent more than their income on things for now, with no thought to the future, with no thought to the *what-ifs* of life. Planning for the *what-ifs* reduces the stress and worry in life. Here are some ways to build a financial cushion to help finance your future goals.

RETIREMENT FUNDS: 401K AND IRA

You're not even 30 yet, why are we talking about retirement? Because if you don't start planning for it while you're young, there won't be any funds to retire with when you want them.

A 401K is a "retirement plan" sponsored by the workplace. An employer sets up the stock/bond program and allows employees to participate. Employees participate by selecting the specific stocks/bonds to be purchased and designating a percentage of their pay to be invested in the selected funds. For example, an employer offers a 401K program that buys shares in stocks A, B, C, and D and bonds K, L, and M. An employee decides to invest a total of 10% of his or her gross pay in A, B, D, and L. Each fund will receive 25% of the 10%. If your monthly gross pay is $2000, each fund would receive $50 ($2000 x 10% = $200, divided by 4 = $50). Usually the selections and percentage designations can be divided up any way you want. There is a limit to the total amount that can be contributed each year; the amount was changed in 2001 to $10,500 per year and goes up each year until 2006 when the maximum amount you can contribute annually will be $15,000.

Some companies offer *matching funds*. This means for every dollar you contribute to the fund, the company will add a specific number of dollars. If you contribute $200 a month, the company may add $10, or $50, or even $200. This will all be explained to you when you get your employment packet. A good question to ask, though, when you are being interviewed for a position is "Does the company offer a 401K program and are there any matching funds?" It will help you to compare the myriad job offers you will receive.

The tricky part about any 401K is that if the money is withdrawn prior to retirement age you have to pay a penalty. There are a few exceptions to this penalty rule: buying a house and medical emergencies. If you change companies you can usually roll-over the 401K; that is, take it with you and put it into some other instrument. Again, talk to an expert before making any decisions about a 401K. Keep in mind, however, that it is an excellent way to save for a future goal. Regardless of how much you contribute each month, any amount will help you prepare for the future. Try to contribute enough to your 401K to be eligible for any matching funds; even if you contribute only 5% of your pay and the company does like-matching, that means your fund will increase by 10%. In light of the inrun 401K problems, keep in mind that it is important to pay close attention to your plan.

If your company doesn't offer a 401K, and it may not, then start your own retirement plan, an IRA. IRA stands for Individual Retirement Account. It was started in the 70s to help people save for retirement, people who did not have retirement plans at work. It has restrictions and penalties similar to those of a 401K. In 2002 you may contribute up to $3,000 a year into an IRA. In 2005 it goes up to $4,000 and in 2008 it will be $5,000. You may start to withdraw from the fund without penalty at age 59 ½.

There are two types of IRAs: the original IRA and the Roth IRA (and maybe more by the time this book is published). With the original one you don't pay taxes on the invested funds until you withdraw the money. With the Roth IRA (named after the senator who thought it up) you pay taxes annually but then the balance is yours tax-free when you withdraw it. Talk to an expert about which way is best for your situation.

Generally you can get an IRA from any company that sells stocks, bonds, or mutual funds and from financial institutions. You can contribute throughout the year or once a year; it makes no difference to the fund; the difference is in how much money you will make with the money you deposit (remember compound interest?). You have until April 15 of the next tax year to make a contribution and be able to claim it on your current tax return. This means, if you put $3,000 into an IRA on April 12, 2003 you can claim it on your 2002 tax return. Please note, your IRA may not be eligible for a tax deduction if your income is too high. Talk to an expert. See Appendix B for a visual representation of how $2,000 can grow over the years; imagine what $3,000 will do!

SAVINGS ACCOUNTS/CERTIFICATES OF DEPOSIT

When starting out, a savings account or money market account at your local financial institution is the best way to start investing. Put money into the account every week; it can be as little as one dollar. The important thing is that you save regularly. Typically savings accounts do not pay high interest rates, but you will not lose your money if the bank fails (if the account is FDIC insured). Think of these accounts as holding accounts, a place to keep your investment money until you have enough to invest in something that pays a better rate of return.

A *certificate of deposit* is a savings account that pays a higher interest rate than a basic savings account, but you have to leave the money in the account for a designated length of time and there is a minimum amount of money required to open the account. You may be able to get a six month CD with a $1,000 minimum paying X%. Or a five year CD with a $500 minimum paying Y%. The amount deposited has to be money you will not need for the designated time period because if you take the money out before the end of the period you will be charged a penalty, usually a hefty penalty.

Savings accounts and money market accounts are a good place to put your money if you think you are going to need it in the not-too-distant-future, like one to five years. Savings and money market accounts are also a good place to keep "ready cash", money that you may need to access quickly in case of an emergency - such as a job layoff. Experts suggest keeping three to six months of living expenses readily accessible to cover you during a life-changing event. Short-term, accessible instruments include savings accounts, CDs, money market accounts, and short-term bonds.

LONG RANGE INVESTING

No, I'm not going to tell you how to make a million in the stock market. Historically, the stock market has shown a profit and is an excellent way to make money **over the long haul.** No one should go into the stock market expecting to make a bundle in a year. Yes, some people do, but it's fairly rare; rare enough that it's still considered *news* when it happens. The stock/bond market is usually a more lucrative alternative to putting your savings into the bank; but it can be more risky also.

Experts will tell you the best method of investing is with a "diversified portfolio". This is the total and varied collection of all your investments: stocks, bonds, real estate, savings accounts, etc. The logical theory is that a diversified portfolio should provide balance; when one (or more) type of investment loses value, the other(s) increase in value. Experts disagree on how much weight to give each type of investment; 50% in stocks with 30% in bonds, and 20% liquid (readily accessible)? 40% in stocks, 40% in real estate and 10% in each bonds and savings accounts? The combinations are endless.

Hundreds of books and almost as many web sites are dedicated to investing. They'll tell you how to invest, why to invest, when to invest, and often where to put your money. Your specific questions can be answered with a few hours of research. But before you start researching, be sure you understand the basics.

I am going to suggest that you consider investing in stocks and/or bonds and/or real estate after careful study and consultation with someone who can teach you about it. However, do not invest the grocery money! Only invest money you can afford to lose.

Let's start with some basic definitions of stocks, bonds, and mutual funds.

Stocks: a share of stock is a partial ownership of a company. When a company wants to raise cash they may sell part of the company to get the money. If Company J sells 10,000 shares and you buy 100 shares, you own 1% of the company. Your ownership entitles you to share in the profits of the company. If the company goes belly-up, you may not get anything.

Money is made in the stock market in two ways: by getting really big *dividends* (profit disbursements) and/or by selling the stock at a higher price than you bought it. The theory in stock purchases is to "buy low, sell high". The tricky part is in deciding when it is high enough or too low. For example, you buy 100 shares of Company J at $15 a share (value = $1500). Two years later the stock is at $25 (value = $2500). At the end of three years, the stock is selling for $38 a share (value = $3800). Is it going to continue to go up or will it go back down? The challenge in the stock market is in the timing and careful monitoring of your portfolio. Keep in mind that most people make money in the stock market over LONG periods of time (five years or more), not in buying and selling on a whim.

Newscasts and periodicals talk about the DOW, NASDAQ, and S&P averages. These reflect the activity in specific groups of stocks. The DOW, otherwise known as the Dow Jones Industrial Average, is the oldest market indicator. The Dow is a composite of 30 blue chip stocks, such as General Electric, General Motors, 3M, and Disney; companies that have been around a long time and are considered mainstays of American industry. The companies included in the index change only rarely. The number reflected in "the Dow" is the total of the closing prices of the companies included in the index, adjusted for splits and dividends.

The S&P, or Standard and Poor's, or S&P 500, tracks the performance of 500 stocks, both large and small companies. It is comprised of 400 industrials, 60 transportation and utility companies, and 40 financial companies. Because of its broader base and weighted value it is considered by some to be the most fair mea-sure of market activity. The S&P is often used as the benchmark when comparing performance of individual stocks, funds, or managers.

The NASDAQ (National Association of Securities Dealers Automated Quotations) —no wonder they went with NASDAQ! — represents about 3500 stocks traded on the domestic over-the-counter market. Generally "Over-the-counter (OTC)" transactions are those securities that are traded via telephone or computer, rather than in person at an exchange. The NASDAQ total reflects performance of the more active OTC shares; those that are better known. This index has been around for about 30 years.

An exchange is simply a locale for buying or selling securities. The New York Stock Exchange (NYSE) was founded in 1792 and reflects activity from Wall Street. The American Stock Exchange (AmEx) reflects activity from the Boston, San Francisco, and Chicago exchanges.

The NASDAQ reflects over-the-counter trading of companies regardless of where the trading occurs. As its name implies, NASDAQ is a computerized system that displays transaction records up-to-the-minute. NASDAQ opened its own headquarters in September 2001. When looking for a particular stock report in the newspaper you need to know where it is traded to find the daily record.

Because of their reputation and accuracy, when all three indexes move in the same direction — up or down — it is considered a trend or a forecast of future economic activity.

Bonds: a bond is basically a loan to a company or government. Bonds are usually sold in increments of $1000 at specific rates of return for a specific period of time. You buy a $1000 bond at 10% for twenty years. That means for the next twenty years you will be paid $100 a year and at the end of the 20 years you get your $1000 back. Some bonds only pay the interest at maturity. Your return will be the same whether the company does great or miserably.

Bonds are sold by corporations and governments (local, state, or federal). You can purchase them through a broker or financial institution or directly from the government. You make money on bonds by purchasing them and holding them to maturity or by selling them for more than the face value before they mature.

Generally, bond prices fluctuate in opposition to the interest rates. When interest rates are low, prices for previously-purchased bonds are high. Let's say you bought a $1000 bond at 9% for 30 years in 1980. In 2001 bonds are selling at 5%. You have been paid $90 a year since the purchase. If you decide to sell your 9% bond, a buyer might offer you $1200 for it because a $1000 8% bond held for (the remaining) nine years is more valuable ($810 in total interest due) than a new $1000 bond at 5% ($50 per year).

Bonds are generally a more conservative method of investing. Federal government bonds (called *Treasuries*) are especially safe because they are backed by the federal government (which we all hope will not default). Local and state bonds (called *Munis*) used to be considered as safe as federal ones, but since the default of Orange County, California, their safety is less assured.

Bonds are rated by companies such as Standard and Poors and Moody's. These ratings reflect the relative safety and stability of the offering. Generally, the greater the risk of the bond (lower rating), the higher the rate being paid to attract investors. Overall, bonds are more stable than stocks; there is less chance of great gains or losses and therefore they are not as profitable as stocks, and there is less risk.

Most bonds provide steady, predictable income, although some can have floating rates. They are especially attractive when saving for a long-range goal such as retirement or your child's education.

Mutual Funds: a mutual fund is a group of stocks, bonds, or both managed by a single company or person. You invest in the specific fund. That fund in turn buys shares in specific stocks and/or bonds. For example, you may invest $200 in the XYZ Mutual Fund. XYZ takes your $200 and the hundreds of dollars of other investors and buys shares in Microsoft, Texaco, Pfizer, and Coca Cola, just to name a few. As an individual you may not be able to afford this variety of shares or very many shares, but as a group the investment is possible. Your return is determined by your percentage of the overall total amount invested.

Mutual funds come in all types. There are those that specialize in one type of investment, such as technology or health products, and there are those that are more general.

You may hear of "loads". A "load" is a commission paid by you to a broker for handling the purchase or sale of a mutual fund. There are front-end and back-end loads, depending on whether it is charged up-front at the purchase, or at the back when the fund is sold. There are also "no-load" funds where no commission is charged and you do all the management of the transactions by yourself.

Mutual funds are a great way to start investing. It is less risky and can be less expensive than trying to invest in one or two "blue chip" (top producing) stocks. Investing $1,000 in XYZ Mutual (or Bond) Fund may provide you more stability and more overall shares than investing $1,000 in individual shares of companies like

Microsoft, Pfizer, or Disney. It is less risky because if one part of the fund's portfolio does poorly, hopefully the other shares will balance it. Most funds have a minimum amount to start investing, but it can be as low as $100.

INVESTING IN STOCKS, BONDS, OR MUTUAL FUNDS

Whether you are thinking of stocks, bonds, or mutual funds as an investment, do your homework. Order the *prospectus* (a pamphlet that explains the product) either by phone or over the Internet. Get advice from people you respect. Deal with a reputable *broker* (seller of stocks/funds/bonds). Check out the Internet or the stock pages of your newspaper to study the recent history of a company or fund you are considering.

Pay attention to what is happening elsewhere in finances because this will affect your investments. When the Fed raises interest rates, loans become less attractive and saving becomes more attractive; when interest rates are low, loans and investing are more attractive. A *bull market* means stock prices are increasing; a *bear market* means stocks are going down.

You can set up an automatic payment plan with many investment companies. This allows a specific amount of money to be taken from each paycheck and invested in stocks or bonds that you have selected.

If you have selected stocks or funds for investment, it is a good idea to enroll in a *dividend reinvestment plan* (DRIP). This means that any dividends paid by a specific stock are used to purchase more of that stock, rather than being sent to you in a check. This is a painless way to increase your portfolio; if you don't see the money you won't spend the money.

Example: You have 25 shares of MNO Company; MNO pays a dividend of 50 cents a share; that's $12.50 to you. You can have them send you a check for $12.50 or use that money to buy more shares of MNO. MNO is selling for $25.00 a share; if you use the DRIP to buy more stock you now have 25 ½ shares. Hopefully the next dividend will be larger and you can acquire more stock. All things being equal, even if the per share dividend is the same (50 cents) your payment will be greater because you now own more shares (25 ½).

See Appendix E for a worksheet to help you make investment comparisons.

STOCK PURCHASE PLANS

Some companies offer a stock purchase plan - sometimes called stock options - for employees, but usually not until you have been with the company for a specific length of time. What this allows you to do is to purchase stock in **that** company at a (possibly) reduced price. If it is a company you trust, you should consider buying the stock. If you don't trust the company, why are you working there?

REAL ESTATE

It is true that, through the ages, real estate has proven to be a safe investment. Generally real estate accrues in value over time. However, there are instances where it has lost value; just as the stock or bond market has down periods. Real estate generally does not accrue value as quickly as other investment forms.

When considering a real estate purchase there are two things to think about. Can I afford the initial costs? And, can I afford the on-going payments? To make a real estate purchase, whether unimproved property (land or a lot), a residential structure, or commercial property, usually requires an initial outlay of cash; it can be 20% of the purchase price or possibly more in the case of commercial property. There are many financing options available for first-time homebuyers that can reduce the amount of the down payment, but you will still need some cash to secure a real estate loan.

Let's assume your first real estate purchase will be for residential purposes. That means you are buying a house, or a condo, or a lot to build on later. When you make the purchase you will need to make monthly payments on the mortgage. The monthly principal and interest payment on a $100,000 mortgage at 7% interest is $665.31 when financed over 30 years, $898.83 when financed over 15 years. You'll have to add taxes and insurance to this amount to get your true monthly payment amount.

In some jobs, such as the government, sales, the military, or some corporate positions, you may move every two or three years. Can you afford to hold onto this property when you have relocated elsewhere? If you sell it when you move, you will have to pay selling costs. If you decide to keep it, will you be able to rent it out? If you rent it out, you will have to pay someone to manage the property for you while you live elsewhere.

Buying a piece of property for future use may be a safer idea than buying a house right away. The problem is in deciding where to buy it. Do you want it somewhere that you live currently or some place where you might like to live someday? Buying for future use is more of a gamble because there are no guarantees what zoning decisions may be made in the future that will affect your property.

In short, if you are considering a real estate purchase talk to a financial expert, not necessarily a real estate agent, and be sure you understand all the present and future aspects of such a purchase. If you decide to make a purchase, enlist the aid of a reputable real estate agent to assist with all the details of the deal.

RULE OF 72

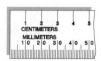

When evaluating investment opportunities, something to keep in mind is the Rule of 72. This investment guideline says that an amount invested will double according to the equation **72 = r x t**, where **r** is the interest rate and **t** is the number of years.

For example, if you invest $1000 at r = 8% it will double in 9 years.

$$72 = 8 \text{ x } 9$$

If you want to know what rate you need to get an investment doubled in 6 years

$$72 = r \text{ x } 6$$
$$r = 12\%$$

The Rule of 72 is a handy tool to use when comparing one investment opportunity to another.

RECORDKEEPING

Keep all records and statements related to your investments. You will need them to pay taxes on any gains you have made or to prove any losses incurred when you finally sell the stock, fund, bond, or real estate. *Capital gains taxes* are paid on any profit you make; if there is a loss you get to take that off your taxes. Different rules apply for each type of invest-  ment so it is a good idea to get professional advice before buying or selling any type of investment property.

THE LAST WORD

There are two secrets to accomplishing your financial goals; have a plan and pay attention to your investments. For some goals, you have to start sooner than for others. If money will be required for any of your goals, the sooner you start the better.

The more responsibilities you have, the harder it is to save. This is not intended as a put-down of marriage and children and home-ownership; it's just a fact of life. The more people involved in any situation, the more *what-ifs* that occur.

The easiets secret is to develop the habit of putting money aside on a regular basis. Have it taken right out of your paycheck and deposited into a savings account, IRA, 401K, or other investment instrument. The amount put aside only matters in the long run, in how

℮—99

much you will have saved over 10 or 20 or 30 years. Start now, save $1.00 a week, $10 a month, or whatever amount you decide you can live with. Save something toward your goals and watch your dreams become realities. See Appendix A.

TIP: Before you go to bed each night put all your change into an empty jar. Don't touch it! At the end of a few months you will be amazed at how much you have saved.

In early 2002 the Enron problems became public. Hundreds of employees lost their life savings when this major corporation reported significant financial irregularities. Many of the employees had their investments tied up in the corporate 401-K plan that invested heavily in Enron stock. For many of these individuals, their whole retirement fund was locked into Enron stock only.

If nothing else, the Enron failure emphasized the need for investors to diversify their holdings and to pay attention to their investements. You should learn how to read and understand corporate reports, watch trends, and learn to rely on your own instincts. Enron showed that even professional investment advisors can be fooled. There is no substitute for the correct information at the right time. You can never learn too much.

Chapter 7

"Budget" Is Not a Four-letter Word

Up to this point we've seen that money is vital to survival, there is a finite amount of it available to you, and credit cards can get you into financial difficulty quickly. Having extra money is a good thing because it can be allowed to grow into even more money. Goal setting helps you achieve your dreams.

So how do you accomplish your goals? It takes money and careful planning to turn goals into realities. The best way to get where you are going, financially, is with a budget. A budget is the road map to your goal.

Think of it this way: you're driving from Bangor, Maine to San Diego, California. Without a map it will take you a lot longer to get there, you may get lost, you may hit detours, you may decide to visit the Alamo or the Grand Canyon. A map keeps you on track and allows you to make the necessary decisions at the appropriate times. Sure, you can drive from Maine to California without a map, but will it be the most direct route? Will you get there on schedule? Of course travelling without a map can be a great adventure, if you have no deadlines or definite destination.

The wonderful thing about a budget is that *you* draw the map. You are the one to decide what direction to take, when you can veer off course to take advantage of unexpected opportunities, and when to drive straight through to the destination. Since it's your map, you get to tweek it, modify it, throw it away and start over if it isn't working. Only you can decide what direction(s) will work for you.

There are some basic steps to follow in developing your budget. Follow these steps and life will be filled with fewer potholes than you could ever imagine. You will have started on the right road and have no bumpy roads or detours to compare it with.

STEP 1: KNOW WHERE YOU'RE COMING FROM

You can't get anywhere if you don't know where the starting point is. If you try to give someone directions to your house, you have to know where their starting point is. Without a starting point directions are useless. That's the same route you need when developing a budget. Get out a pencil and paper or your PC and get started. You can even do this using software like *Quicken*™, but it has more impact if you do it on paper the first time.

Income

What is your current net income? Do you have a job? Do you have an inheritance? Allowance from the folks? Stock dividends? Savings bonds? Alimony? Child support?

Determine your *monthly* net income. If you get a lump sum lottery pay-out each year, divide that amount by 12 to get the average monthly amount. If your paycheck varies each month take two (or three or four) months' pay statements, add them together and divide by two (or three or four).

If you are creating a budget for post-graduation, use your expected/hoped for income. Remember to allow for local, state, and federal taxes, Social Security, and Medicare being deducted. If these items are not automatically deducted from your gross pay, you need to deduct them and set them aside; the remaining amount is your *net income*, your spending money, disposable income, discretionary funds. In short, the remainder is what you have to live on until the next pay period.

TIP: Always work from your *net income*, not gross. The automatic deductions are never seen and go to pay one kind of tax or another, so don't even consider them in the budget.

Okay, that's the easy part, and the quickest. Now let's see where the money goes. Plan on two budgets, one for right now, and one as a future budget.

Current Expenses

List all your expenses and how much you spend on each. For most undergraduates, your expenses, outside of tuition, housing, and books, are fairly easy to identify: laundry, clothing, entertainment, food, maybe transportation. Figuring out how much you spend on each may not be so easy.

The best (and most time-consuming) way to determine how much you spend is to keep a log. You can use your checkbook register for part of it. Write down *everything* you spend money on. That means everything! You buy a Coke™ out of a vending machine, write it down. You put quarters into the washing machine, write it down. You go to a movie, write it down. You buy snacks at the grocery, write it down. Get receipts when possible. Do this record-keeping for one month, two would be better. Save ALL your notes and receipts.

At the end of the time period, divide the itemized expenses into categories. Some sample categories might be

- Laundry/Dry Cleaning
- Loans (car, credit cards, parents, other)
- Gifts - don't forget little brother's birthday
- Postage/shipping
- Clothing
- Entertainment (movies, ball games, meals out, etc.)
- Telephone - call home!
- Transportation(gas for the car, mass transit, car insurance, etc.)
- Food (outside of any pre-paid meal plan at school)
- Tuition (if you are paying this, not someone else)
- Room and board (if you are paying this, not someone else)
- Books (if you are paying this, not someone else)
- Refrigerator/microwave rental
- Insurance(s)

Divide your log notes, checks, and receipts into the necessary categories. Total the amounts. Surprise! Those french fries mount up, don't they? For some other examples of accumulated expenses, see Appendix D.

If you have some expenses that occur only once or twice a year (like car insurance), be sure to include them in your list of expenses.

You now have a total of your current expenses. If you kept track for a month, use this figure as your average monthly expense. If it's an annual expense, divide the annual figure by 12 to get the monthly average. Write the monthly figures in the spaces provided on the worksheet at the end of this chapter.

Expenses - Post Graduation/Future

If you haven't started thinking about what it's going to cost you to live after graduation, there's no time like the present. If you don't start thinking about it now, how are you going to afford it then? Getting a job may be the least of your worries when you enter the "real world".

Some typical start-up expenses that you will face are:

- Rent - initial security deposit, monthly lease, possibly the first month's rent in advance
- Utilities - gas, electricity, phone, water (you are going to shower and call home aren't you?); initial connection charges
- Insurance - car, health, renter's, life
- Transportation - gas, repairs/upkeep, mass transit
- Laundry/dry cleaning
- Groceries - food, toiletries
- Medicine - doctors, prescriptions
- Student loan paybacks - these usually start six months after graduation
- Other loans - car, parents, credit cards
- Gifts
- Furnishings for the new residence - furniture, small appliances, dishes, linens, toilet paper, bath soap, toothpaste
- Postage/shipping - don't forget Mom's birthday!

Guesstimate how much each of these will cost. Use the worst case scenario. Come up with average monthly expenses for each item, just as we did for your current expenses. Fill in the worksheet; it's okay to photocopy it so you have extras to work with; you'll need them.

STEP 2: KNOW WHERE YOU ARE GOING

Somewhere along the way you should have set some goals for yourself. Now come up with a dollar amount for those goals. If you want to go to Europe after graduation, how much is it going to cost? If you want two kids (someday), how much will it cost to send them to college? If you want to retire at 40, how much will you need to have saved to do so?

These things may seem a long way off, but the time to start thinking about them is now, or they will never become a reality. Ask your parents.

One reason most people get into financial stress is because they fail to do any long-range planning. It's actually fairly painless if you start by deducting for one or more long range goals with your first paycheck.

Now add your goals and their estimated costs to your list of expenses. If the trip to Europe is going to cost $12,000 and you graduate in two years, you need to save $500 a month to meet your goal. Hmmmm.

Plan to buy a house some day? You may need a down payment. Down payments can run as high as 20% of the sales price of the house. On a $100,000 house, that's $20,000. If you think you'll be ready for a house in ten years, that's $2,000 a year to put aside. Of course in ten years houses may cost more, but that's another story. You may be able to put down less, but then your monthly note will be higher. Plus, if you put down less than 20% then you have to pay mortgage insurance which increases your monthly note even more, but that's another whole book! Relax, there are all kinds of programs to help first-time home buyers, but you **will** need some kind of ready cash to buy a house.

Add a line in your list of expenses for EMERGENCIES. This is a contingency fund to cover the *unexpected*. It could be a trip to your best friend's wedding, a medical emergency, a new car, a faster computer, or job interview expenses.

Add one more line to your list of expenses: SAVINGS/ INVESTMENTS. Start right now paying yourself first. We talked in the last chapter about investments. You will never have any money to invest if you do not start setting something aside out of every check. There is no hard and fast rule about how much to put aside, the important thing is to put something aside out of every check; it can be one dollar, five dollars, one hundred dollars. You set the amount; make it something you can live with. If you make yourself feel deprived, you won't stick to it. Try to put aside 20% - 30% of your net income each month. Review the interest compounding examples in Appendix A.

Future Value Formula

To determine how much a specific dollar amount will be worth in the future, use this formula

$$V = D(1+A) \, t$$

V = the future value

D = your initial deposit, in whole dollars

A = the interest rate being paid (APR or APY), in decimal form

T = the length of time invested, in years

Example: You deposit $5,000 into an account with simple interest at 6.5% and leave it there for one year. The value at the end of that one year will be $5,325 ($5,000 x [1+.065]).

You invest $5,000 into a mutual fund at 6.5% interest and leave it there for five years. The value at the end of that five years will be

$$V = 5000 \ (1 + .065)^5$$
$$= 5000 \ (1.065)5$$
$$= 5000 \ (1.37008666341)$$
$$= 6850.43 \ \text{(rounded)}$$

Many calculators and Internet sites will do this for you if you plug in the appropriate numbers. Use these figures with the worksheet in Appendix E.

STEP 3: WORK WITH ME

Using each set of forms (current and future) at the end of this chapter total all your income items and come up with a *total average monthly income.* Total all your expenses and come up with a *total average monthly expenses* figure.

Compare the two totals. If your income is greater than your expenses, YEA! Most likely it's the other way around. Now what?

There are only two ways to remedy this situation: increase your income and/or decrease your expenses. In reality, the easiest (and least fun) is to reduce your expenses. Look at your notes and receipts. Is there anything you can cut out? Fewer Cokes™? Less expensive apartment? Bathe once a week in cold water? Can you go to Europe in four years instead of two? Rent movies instead of going to them? Or go to cheaper movie showings?

Look carefully at your grocery receipts. Anything there you can do without? Read magazines at the library instead of buying them?

Buy bread and deli meats and make your own sandwiches instead of ready-made deli sandwiches? Buy Cokes™ in cartons or two liter bottles instead of out of vending machines? Be creative!

Work with these lists until your monthly income and expenses are in balance. Then, using a blank worksheet, fill in your *budgeted* amount for each item. The nice thing about your time of life is that your income should keep increasing for the next twenty to forty years and your expense items will stay semi-stable (unless you move a lot, buy a house, or have a family). The trick is to learn to set a budget and **stick to it**. It does no good to go to this time and effort to come up with a budget and then ignore it. It's like buying every map you can find and leaving them in the trunk while you drive cross-country.

STEP 4: REVIEW, MODIFY AND STICK TO IT

Even after your budget is set, keep tracking and recording your expenses. Compare them with your budget quarterly. Tweek as necessary.

Annually, thoroughly review your budget. Hopefully you will have received a raise at work, or found a new job, or have won the lottery. At this time in your life, your income should be increasing fairly regularly. You need to adjust your budget accordingly for the next year.

Any time you get a raise, increase the amount you are setting aside for your goals and investments by at least 30% of the net raise amount. If the net increase in your monthly pay is $100 a month, put $30 of that into your GOAL(S) and SAVINGS/INVESTMENTS line items. Hey, you were getting along without it before you got the raise; you can get along without it now. You still have an additional $70 a month to put toward a new apartment, new car, more nights out, more gifts for Mom, or more whatever.

That's one of the biggest secrets to this whole budget thing. Don't make it hurt. Give yourself a real raise, have more fun, but don't overlook the long-range plans. If you stretch the budget so tight that you are sitting in every night staring at the walls because you can't afford to go out, you won't stick to the budget. Have an ENTERTAINMENT item in your budget, allow yourself to have fun. Just stick to the budget.

An easy way to get used to sticking to the budget is the old envelope trick. When you get your paycheck, divvy it up into different envelopes: gas, groceries, entertainment, etc. When the money's gone from that envelope, you stop spending on that item. Or you borrow money from another envelope, knowing that you are reducing the amount you can spend on that item instead. You are making informed decisions about how to spend your money. You may prefer to buy two big juicy steaks and a strawberry shortcake and eat in this week rather than going out; the grocery envelope can't afford it, but the entertainment one can. It's your decision. Once you are in the habit of following your budget you can throw away the envelopes.

That is the glory of a budget. It puts you in control of your finances and your life. You know what your income is, what your expenses are, what your future expenses are, you are prepared for unexpected expenses, and you can make informed decisions. Too cool!

CURRENT BUDGET WORKSHEET

Total Average Monthly Income(net, after deductions) $_____(1)

Average Fixed Monthly Expenses (in no particular order)

Housing (if you are paying it)	$_____
Food (if you are paying it)	$_____
Tuition (if you are paying it)	$_____
Transportation (auto fuel, service, mass transit)	$_____
Insurance (auto, renter's)	$_____
Utilities (gas, electricity, phone, water)	$_____
Debts (loans, credit card debts)	$_____
Medical/Dental	$_____
Savings/Investments	$_____
Emergencies	$_____
Charitable contributions	$_____
Refrigerator/microwave rental	$_____

Subtotal $_____(2)

Average Variable Monthly Expenses (in no particular order)

Entertainment	$_____
Gifts	$_____
Clothing	$_____
Laundry/Dry cleaning	$_____
Postage/shipping	$_____
Books/supplies	$_____
Other	$_____

Subtotal $_____(3)

Total Average Monthly Expenses ([2] + [3]) $_____(4)

Income (1) minus Expenses (4) = $_____ *

Note (3): these items are not fixed expenses so they can be reduced the easiest
*This is the amount left to put toward your goal(s)

FUTURE BUDGET WORKSHEET

Total Average Monthly Income (net, after deductions) $_____ (1)

Average Fixed Monthly Expenses (in no particular order)

Housing (deposit, monthly note)	$_____
Groceries (food, toiletries)	$_____
Tuition (grad school?)	$_____
Transportation (auto fuel, service, mass transit)	$_____
Insurance (auto, renter's, health, life)	$_____
Utilities (gas, electricity, phone, water)	$_____
Debts (loans, credit card debts)	$_____
Medical/Dental	$_____
Savings/Emergencies	$_____
Charitable contributions	$_____
Goal 1	$_____
Goal 2	$_____
Subtotal	$_____

Average Variable Monthly Expenses (in no particular order)

Entertainment	$_____
Gifts	$_____
Clothing	$_____
Laundry/Dry cleaning	$_____
Postage/shipping	$_____
Furnishings	$_____
Other	$_____
Subtotal	$_____ (3)

Total Average Monthly Expenses ([2] + [3]) $_____ (4)

Income (1) minus Expenses (4) = $_____ *

Note (3): these items are not fixed expenses so they can be manipulated the easiest

Chapter 8

The A-B-C's of Making Money Work for You

Avoid temptation. This means if you have a weakness for malls, don't go to the mall. If you never met a Hallmark® card you didn't like, stay out of card shops. Don't put yourself in the path of temptation; reduce your opportunities to spend money.

Analyze your current situation. Know how you are spending money now; then determine what you can live without. See chapter 7.

Avoid book/CD/video clubs. Don't even look at those offers that come in the mail and in the Sunday papers! How much could you save by buying the same book/CD/video at the local store?

ATM fees can mount up quickly. Try to use the ATM at machines owned by your parent bank. If you use the ATM for spending money, get a lump sum each week, all at once, rather than running back to the machine multiple times during the week.

Automatic withdrawals make saving and investing easier. Automatic withdrawals can be created to move money automatically from your checking or savings account to more lucrative investment instruments.

Backup is critical. If you are keeping any of your financial records on a computer, be sure you backup the data at least *quarterly*.

Budget. Think of a budget as a tool to a better life, the roadmap to stress-free living. See chapter 7.

Keep the Big Picture in mind. Remember, a single can of Coke™ may not cost much, but a can a day for 365 days can mount up. Could you find a better use for that $300?

Bankruptcy can affect your ability to get credit for up to ten years. It is not the debt end-all it used to be considered.

Buy store brands. If you can get the same quality of product —whether it's toilet paper or polo shirts— without a "name brand" or logo and for less money, why pay more for something just because it has recognition factor? If you're worried about what your friends will think, think about THAT!

Bill consolidation *may* be a good way to get out of debt more quickly. Determine if you can make one monthly payment at a lower interest rate and thereby get your debts paid off faster.

Clip coupons. It may seem silly, but if you can save a dime here, a quarter there, it will mount up after a while. Look for stores that offer "double coupons" and save even more.

Compound interest is your best friend. When making any type of investment (savings account, stock purchase, or IRA) be sure the interest is being compounded. This way you get interest on the interest. Just remember, interest is compounded on credit card balances, too, so pay off your credit card debts as quickly as possible.

Create new habits. Post your goals and your budget in obvious places: bathroom mirror, refrigerator door, in your wallet or checkbook. That way every time you consider an expenditure you will be reminded of the big picture.

Comparison shop. Whether looking for a new car or a new toothbrush, compare prices of similar items. Buy the best quality you can afford that meets your needs; it doesn't have to meet your neighbor's approval.

Credit reports should be ordered annually and checked for accuracy. See Chapter 5.

Communicate with your family so everyone is working on the same game plan. If you are living in a family situation (more than just you) discuss your plans. When everyone is working toward the same goal, it will be accomplished even sooner. Make a game of saving money; who can save the most money this week? Who can find new ways to save money?

Disposable income is not really disposable. It's only "disposable" because it is not required to meet a NEED. There is always a use for "leftover" money. A good use is to save it for the future.

DRIPs can make your money grow faster. Dividend Reinvestment Plans are a form of compounding. When a stock pays a dividend, those funds can be reinvested in the stock automatically, before you have a chance to spend the money otherwise. This increases your investment in that stock or fund without you having to think about it.

Debt is a function of expenses, not of income. Use a budget to manage your income, to understand where the money is going, and your debt load will be minimal.

Don't be afraid to ask questions.

Direct deposit is the best way to go. Have your paycheck automatically deposited to your bank account. It is safer and faster than having to carry around a paper check to deposit when you find the time.

Don't make payments late. Most companies —from credit cards to utilities - charge a late fee when payments do not arrive by the deadline. This is just extra cash out of your pocket. Write out your bill payments and put the due date in the corner of the envelope (where the stamp goes). Mail the payment to arrive at least one day before the due date.

Emergencies happen to everyone. Plan for them. Have an account at the bank where you keep at least $500 for emergencies; this should be enough liquidity to see you through most emergencies until you can sell some stock or cash in other investments to cover major emergencies. Maintain a major credit card, too, *for emergency use only.*

Evaluate your current expenses. Review your budget and expenses every month. Adjust as needed.

Empty pockets before doing laundry. You'll be amazed at how much change, and even dollar bills, can be found in pockets.

Fun is important. Don't budget until it hurts; you won't stick to it. Be sure your budget includes an amount for entertainment.

Money comes in a Finite amount, it doesn't grow on trees nor fall from the sky. Your income is your income, you can augment it with appropriate investments, but you can't turn $100 into $1000 by wishing it was so.

Follow maintenance instructions. When you buy a car or a major appliance, follow the maintenance instructions. This should keep the item usable for a longer period of time and keep you from having to buy a replacement.

FDIC is a good thing. This stands for Federal Deposit Insurance Corporation. When an account is "FDIC-insured" that means your risk is lowered, your deposits are insured up to a specific amount, usually $100,000. Verify that your bank accounts are insured this way and that you understand any limitations.

Goals give you purpose. Write them down. Keep them handy. Review them every morning.

Give yourself a raise. When your boss gives you a raise, give yourself one by increasing some budget amounts. Put at least 30% of every raise into your savings/investment accounts. That leaves you 70% for food, entertainment, or even a new apartment.

Group errands. Save gas by running errands at one time. Rather than going out to run one errand four times a week, run four errands on one day.

Get leverage with your banker. The more accounts and the more money you have at one bank, the more the bank will be willing to work with you when you need to borrow money or have a problem resolved.

Hold on to what you've got. Just because you have money in your pocket (or checking account) doesn't mean you have to spend it. Sometimes it makes more sense to save $10 a month and buy a $200 piece of furniture rather than rush out and buy a $50 piece.

Hope for the best, plan for the worst. If you maintain a healthy balance between saving and spending your life will be less stressful.

Homework isn't just for school. Research products before you buy them, investments before you make them, loans before you take them. Read all contracts and agreements completely before accepting them.

Invest in an IRA or 401K as soon as possible. These are excellent tools for retirement planning. Traditionally their interest compounding features are among the best in the investment world.

Identity theft can happen to anyone. Do the best you can to limit identity theft. See Chapter 4.

Information is power.

Jump at the chance to put money aside for future goals. If you get a bonus or an inheritance or a lottery winning, don't blow it, save a big part of it. You were getting along without it before weren't you?

Kick old habits. See Avoid Temptation above.

Keep big bills in your wallet, you're less likely to spend them. If you're carrying around cash, keep it in $20 or higher denominations for as long as possible. Seeing the big bills will remind you of your budget and your goals.

Keep a money jar. Trite, but true. Those pennies mount up, as in "a penny saved is a penny earned", "waste not want not".

Keep tags on purchased items. If you buy a new suit or a gift for someone, don't take the tags off until you are really ready to wear/wrap the item. You may change your mind about the purchase; if the tags are still on it usually you can return it with less hassle.

Look around for investment opportunities. Do your homework. Read financial magazines and research on the Internet.

Libraries are great sources of free material. Read *Money* magazine or use the Net at your local library. Read any magazine at the library and save the subscription price. Check out books rather than buying them. Many libraries loan music and videos.

Loan-to-debt ratios are only guidelines. Lenders look for an overall ratio of about 36% when making loans. That means your debt load cannot exceed 36% of your gross income. In reality, that's a heavy load. Be sure you can live with your own loan-to-debt ratio and still have a life.

Mutual funds. When in doubt about which stock(s) to purchase, look into mutual funds. They can provide a more balanced method of investing with less risk than a single-stock/bond purchase.

Make friends with yourself. Don't punish yourself for planning ahead. Reward yourself whenever you meet a milestone in your great plan. Think positively about your budget; take pride in using one.

Moderation is the key. Don't starve yourself or bore yourself because you are trying to stick to your budget. If the budget hurts, make adjustments to it to make it more livable.

 et income is "real" money. Remember to live on your net income, after taxes, social security and Medicare have been deducted.

Need vs. want. When making any purchase, ask yourself if this is a need or a want. Needs are vital to survival, wants are not. Some wants are vital to happiness however.

No cheating. Stick to your budget. Be honest with yourself.

ff-season purchases can save you money. Buy lawn-mowers at the end of summer, skis at the end of winter, and bathing suits at the Fourth of July sales. Appliances and cars usually go on sale in January and August.

Overdraft protection may be cheaper than NSF fees. If not, with it you at least avoid the returned check fees.

Open a savings account to start investing. Most investments require a minimum amount to open an account. Put money aside in a savings account while you build toward the higher-paying investments.

Prioritize. Once you know how much money you have, and what your needs are, you can prioritize everything else in your financial life. Is it more important to buy a new suit or to put that money into your vacation fund? Do you need a new car this year or can you save for a new house?

Pay promptly. Pay all bills in full each month. If you cannot, send the payment as soon as possible. Most creditors, especially credit card companies, charge interest on outstanding balances and on new purchases if the previous month's bill was not paid in full. The sooner you reduce the outstanding balance, the less interest you will be charged.

Pay yourself first. When you get a paycheck, immediately put part of it aside for savings/investments. Live off what's left.

Peace of mind is delightful. Living within your means will allow you to sleep at night and get through each day without worrying where the money's going to come from.

Pay off high-interest debts first. If you already have a heavy debt load, determine which debts are costing you the most, which ones have the highest interest rates. Pay as much as you can on these while paying the minimum on the lower-interest accounts.

Quicken™ is a great way to track and plan your funds. If you are computerized, spend about $50 to get your budget and investments digitized using Quicken™ software. It makes your expense-tracking, bill-paying, and investment-history almost automatic.

Quit whining. Remember, no pain, no gain. It may hurt for a while, but in a fairly short time frame your new lifestyle will become habit and your savings will be so great that you'll be celebrating rather than whining.

Question every purchase. Ask yourself "is this something I need?", "how will this purchase affect my attainment of my goal(s)?", "can I wait for this until next week/month/year?", "is this in my budget?"

Retirement isn't as far off as you think. People are making life changes in their fifties rather than their sixties these days. Will you be ready?

Read *The Millionaire Next Door*. It will encourage you to save for the important things in life and to see that you CAN do it.

Reduce expenses. Look for ways to cut expenses. Go to afternoon movies, buy soda in cartons rather than vending cans, vacation at home one year, learn to cut your own hair. The ideas are only limited by your imagination.

Reward yourself. Set milestones. "When we open an investment account, we'll go out for a big dinner."

"When we have half the money saved for a house down payment, we'll buy a lamp for the house."

Read the fine print of any agreement/contract/lease before you sign it.

Renter's insurance should not be optional. Many people say "I don't have anything worth insuring"; it's not so much the value of the items as the replacement costs if anything happens to them. How much would it cost to replace everything you own - clothes, computer, dishes, sheets, towels, toothpaste, etc.?

Stocks and bonds are for the long haul. These should be considered as long-term investments, meaning five years or more, preferably ten years or more. If you can't afford to do without the money for that long, don't put it into stocks or bonds.

Save some amount of money every month. Put something aside every month. It's the one most important habit you should create. The regularity is as important as the amount.

Save receipts. Keep receipts for every major purchase - over $25. Keep them for at least one year or until the warranty period is up.

Set a good example. If you have children, living within your means is the best thing you can teach them. Explain about budgets, spending, and saving, too.

Shop at sales. Whether it's the grocery or the department store, watch for items on sale. Don't buy something just because it's on sale, but if it's something you need, or will need in the near future, buy it when you can get it for less.

Speak up! If you detect an error or a problem with any of your finances, get to the bottom of it.

Start NOW. There's no time like the present to get your finances in order.

Status symbols; are they worth it? If a Saturn meets your needs, why buy a Lexus? Unless you plan on a large family or entertaining a lot, will you need a 5,000 square foot house? Can you play better golf in a Tommy Hilfiger™ polo shirt than in a K-Mart store brand?

Tear up all extraneous credit cards. Keep the minimum number of cards, for safety and financial concerns. The more you carry, the more chances there are for identity theft and for you to be tempted to use them. Keep one major credit card for emergencies.

Taxes should be paid, but don't pay more than you are required to do. Figure your taxes carefully; use a program like TurboTax™ if you're doing your taxes by yourself. If your taxes are complicated, hire a reputable CPA. Not paying taxes can land you in jail and with heavy financial penalties.

Use a list when shopping. Trying to wing it when you're shopping leads to over-buying and impulse buying.

Used cars (pre-owned) are less expensive than new. New cars lose a large part of their value when they are driven out of the dealership. Buying a car that's one or two years old with low mileage may be a better investment than buying a new car. But you lose that new-car smell. Loan interest may be higher than for a new car, so do the arithmetic.

Visualize success. Every step of the way, picture yourself enjoying the fruits of your financial strategy. Whether you want to retire to Tahiti, buy your own business, put your kids through college, or myriad other adventures, picture yourself succeeding (reclining on the beach, studying the company's bottom line, beaming at graduation) and you're more likely to stick to your plan.

Watch your money grow. Review your finances each quarter. Pat yourself on the back as your balances grow.

Willpower is the secret. You are the only one who can be strict with yourself. If you want to succeed, you have to be self-directed. If in a family situation, everyone has to cooperate for success to be achieved.

Withholding. Make sure your withholding amount is set correctly. Don't have so many deductions claimed that you owe lots of taxes, or so few claimed that the government gets your money interest-free for a year.

Wait 24 hours before making a major purchase. Whether it's a new sofa or a new house, hold off for 24 hours. Think the purchase through very thoroughly; this will help avoid buyer's remorse. Buyer's remorse is when you make a purchase and then start second-guessing yourself after the fact.

e**X**ercise your imagination to find ways to cut your expenses. Get kids involved. Children are very creative at this sort of thing.

You're in control. It's your money and your life. You have no one to answer to except yourself (at least until you have a family). If you get your finances in control now, they will be in control for the rest of your life.

Pretend you're a **Z**ebra - keep everything in black and white. Maintain written records of your budget, expenses, investments, taxes, and anything else related to finances.

Chapter 9

Your Future is Now

Well, that's it. You should be ready now to do more research and ask intelligent questions about those areas where you have special interests. Whether your future is as a statesman, plumber, cab driver, journalist, or whatever you should be better prepared to enter into that field. At a young age it is hard to see too far into the future, it seems so far away.

As I have tried to show in this book, the future, with all its opportunities and challenges, is sooner than you think. Your next car loan, a mortgage on a house, a wedding, children, and your retirement will be upon you before you know it. If you don't at least give these things a cursory thought right now, they will hit you like a ton of bricks when they do happen.

In mid-2001, the median price for an existing home in the U.S. was $152,600. To avoid mortgage insurance and its increased monthly note, you need to make a down payment of 20% ($30,520). Closing costs (the expenses of buying a house) run about 3 - 4% of the loan amount (.035 x $122,080 = $4,272). Think about it.

Five important things you should have learned from this little book: a budget is your friend, save something every month, debt is a heavy burden to carry around with you, debt is a function of expenses not of income, and a good credit report will serve you well through life.

These things work together. With a budget you will be able to save something every month, you will not allow yourself to take on too much debt, and by staying out of serious debt you will maintain a pristine credit report. A good credit rating will allow you to apply for lower interest rates when the time comes to take out those major loans in the future.

Only you can control your spending and saving habits. Be sure the habits you develop now are the ones you need for the rest of your life.

Don't be afraid to ask "what if?" or any other question that gets you an answer. By asking you are no worse off than you were before, and at least you have an answer. Not knowing creates stress and stressed-out is no way to live.

I wish you the best in your future!

[13] Source: Virginia Association of Realtors, "Virginia Home Sales Still Hot", June, 2001

GLOSSARY

APR or APY - Annual Percentage Rate or Annual Percentage Yield; the amount of interest to be paid over the course of a year.

Audit - a review of something; when used with tax audit it refers to the review of one or more year's tax returns.

Automated Teller Machine (ATM) - a computerized machine which allows customers to perform banking transactions 24 hours a day.

Bear market - refers to the stock market when stock prices have a downward trend.

Blocking - the practice of reserving funds for a specific payment via a debit or credit card; especially used by gasoline, hotel, and rental car companies.

Bond - an investment that reflects the loan of a certain amount of money to a government or company; it is repaid with interest at a designated future date.

Bounced check - a check returned to the payee when there are not enough funds in the account to cover the amount of the check.

Broker- an intermediary; one who facilitates the buying or selling of property such as real estate, stocks, and bonds.

Bull market - refers to the stock market when stock prices have an upward trend.

Buyer's remorse - the common feeling a buyer gets after a major purchase wondering "Did I pay too much?"; sometimes referred to as second-guessing yourself.

Carrier - an organization providing insurance, as in "insurance carrier".

Cleared - reflects the transference of money from one account to another; when used with a check —"the check has cleared"— it means the money has been received from the writer of the check.

Clearinghouse - an intermediary that facilitates the transfer of money between banks.

Compound interest - the practice of paying interest on top of interest; when an account receives interest "compounded daily" that means the APR is divided into daily increments, the next day's interest is then paid based on the new sum of the original amount plus the daily interest.

Credit card company - the type of credit card (American Express, Visa, MasterCard, Discover).

Credit card issuer - the financial company that provides the credit card to the customer and to which the bills are paid.

Credit history - a record of all public financial transactions.

Credit report - a report of the credit history of an individual.

Credit scoring - a grading of an individual's credit history, providing a relative position of the individual as related to other individuals with the same type history.

Debit card - a plastic card issued by financial institutions to facilitate payment at point-of-sale locations; operates similar to a check but has the convenience of a credit card.

Debt - an amount owed.

Deductible - an amount, usually calculated annually, that an insurance policy holder must pay before the insurance company begins payments.

Deductions - amounts removed from something, as in a paycheck; *taxes are deducted from a paycheck* and the net amount is then paid to the employee.

Default - failure to pay.

Demand Deposit Account - an account at a financial institution that requires immediate payment; checking account or money market account.

Deposit - the input of funds to an account.

Discretionary Funds - funds not designated for a specific purpose.

Disposable Income - funds not designated for a specific purpose.

Dividend - a sum or fund to be divided among members; as in a stock dividend - cash or additional shares of stock are distributed among stockholders.

DRIP - Dividend Reinvestment Plan. Any stock dividends are automatically re-deposited into the plan by purchasing additional shares in the plan.

Expenses - those things that require money to be spent.

Fed - The Federal Reserve Board. The organization responsible for maintaining the monetary direction of the United States.

Finance charge - interest applied by financial institutions and credit card issuers for the use of funds.

Float - the time between when a check is written and when it clears.

Gross income - the contracted amount being paid to an employee. The amount reported to the Internal Revenue Service.

Inflation - the trend of rising prices.

Income - money received.

Income tax - an annual fee paid to one or more government entities to cover the cost of services provided by that government; it is a percentage of the amount of money earned in the preceding year.

Individual Retirement Account (IRA) - a retirement account set up by an individual; deposits and withdrawals are regulated by the federal government.

Insurance - contracted coverage against loss caused by a specific incident or event.

Interest - an amount paid for the use of funds.

Late fees - a fee applied by financial institutions and credit card issuers for the late payment of a loan.

Loan - an amount borrowed.

Loan-to-debt ratio - a mathematical guide used by those offering loans to determine how much total debt a borrower can handle.

Long-term capital gains - the profit earned on investments held more than one year. Taxes on long-term capital gains are less than those on short-term gains.

Money - a medium of exchange; you exchange three dollars for a box of cereal.

Mutual fund - an investment of the funds of multiple people in one or more stock or bond holdings.

Need - anything necessary for survival.

Net income - the amount of money received from an outside source after all deductions have been taken.

NSF - not (or non) sufficient funds; a condition in which an account does not have enough funds to cover a draft presented for payment from the account.

Overdraw - to take more funds from a financial account than are actually in the account.

Payee - the person to whom a check is written.

Portfolio - all investment holdings of an individual.

Posted - the act of recording transactions (deposits and withdrawals) to an account.

Premium - the periodic payment on an insurance policy.

Prime rate - the interest rate provided to the most credit-worthy customers of a financial institution.

Principal - the amount of an investment; the original amount of a loan.

Prospectus - printed information about a company that is provided to prospective investors.

Rate - the amount paid or charged for the use of funds, as in interest rate.

Repossession - the act of retrieving a property because of non-payment of a debt.

Reserves - the amount banks must keep on-hand to cover current deposits; the amounts are defined by the Federal Reserve Board.

Short-term capital gains - profit acquired on investments held less than one year. Taxes on short-term gains are usually higher than those paid on long-term gains.

Source of Funds - where money comes from.

Stock - the paper reflecting an investment in a company; or the inventory of a company.

Time Deposit Account - an account in which the funds are left for a period of time in order to increase in value, for example savings accounts, CDs.

Use of Funds - the method by which monies are paid out.

Vested - the length of time (usually of employment) before certain actions may be taken. For example, it takes ten years to get vested in the company and be eligible for the stock options.

Want - a strong desire.

Withholding - an amount deducted from payment, often for advance payment of taxes.

EXAMPLES OF COMPOUND INTEREST

Future value of $100 invested monthly, at the beginning of each month with interest compounded monthly (rounded).

Year	5% Interest	8% Interest	15% Interest
1	$1,338	$1,361	$1,418
2	$2,639	$2,728	$2,948
3	$4,007	$4,207	$4,724
5	$6,957	$7,546	$9,179
10	$15,758	$18,639	$28,310
20	$41,546	$59,787	$153,567

Future value of a single $1,000 deposit

Year	5% Interest	8% Interest	15% Interest
1	$1,051	$1,183	$1,161
2	$1,104	$1,173	$1,347
3	$1,161	$1,270	$1,564
5	$1,283	$1,490	$2,107
10	$1,647	$2,220	$4,440
20	$2,713	$4,926	$19,715

Calculations courtesy of webwinder.com

TIME IS MONEY; THE GROWTH OF
$2000

The chart below shows the compounded effect of an annual deposit of $2,000 at various interest rates, assuming deposits start at different ages. The total shown is adjusted for a predicted inflation rate of 4%, which may or may not be accurate between now and when you turn 65.*

| First Deposit | | Accumulation at age 65 | | |
Age	Total Deposited	10% rate	12% rate	15% rate
18	$96,000	$292,266.41	$581,867.92	$1,660,750.72
22	88,000	232,400.61	431,517.59	1,109,810.41
30	72,000	145,775.69	236,097.02	494,328.63
40	52,000	78,761.37	108,447.66	177,251.32
50	32,000	38,387.71	45,652.65	59,496.03
60	12,000	12,195.52	12,827.10	13,836.41

NOTE: $2000 a year is $167 a month (rounded) or $42 a week (rounded).

Calculations courtesy of Quicken.

CREDIT CARD PAYMENT EXAMPLES

Generally, credit card companies require a minimum payment each month. The common minimum amount is 2% of the outstanding balance.

First bill/Initial debt:	$5000	
1st minimum payment (2%)	$ 100	
Second bill	$4965.32	includes new finance charge ($4900 x .01333)
2nd minimum payment (2%)	$ 99	($99.31 rounded to $99)
Third bill	$4931.19	includes new finance charge ($4866.32 x .01333)

You've paid almost $200 and your debt has gone down almost $70. The debt reduction slows down from here. At this 16% interest rate, it will take more than 35 years to pay off this $5000 debt by paying 2% each month IF no new charges are added to the card and no late fees are acquired.

That includes $9,329 in interest over the 35 years
2% minimum drops from $100 each month
1.3333% interest charged per month

At 18% interest, it will take 46 years.

Simple math, payback if no interest charges were applied

$5000 / $100 = 50 payments; 4 years and 2 months

Want to check the repayment time on your credit card debt? Go to **www.webwinder.com** or **www.myvesta.org**

Sample total debt payments, assuming only the minimum is paid each month*

Original Debt	Interest Rate	Total Time	Total Payment(P&I)
$1,000	12%	11.58 years	$1,696.62
$1,000	16%	15.58 years	$2,329.44
$1,000	18%	19.33 years	$2,931.11
$2,200	12%	18.17 years	$4,096.60
$2,200	16%	25.42 years	$5,929.44
$2,200	18%	32.42 years	$7,731.12
$5,000	12%	24.92 years	$9,696.61
$5,000	16%	35.66 years	$14,329.44
$5,000	18%	46 years	$18,931.11

*Calculations courtesy of webwinder.com

IT MOUNTS UP!

	Individual Cost	Annual Cost
ATM Fees	not your bank, $2.00 per week	$104
Soft Drink	$.75 per can, five a week	$195
Lottery Ticket	$4 a week	$208
Movie	two people, matinee, with popcorn and a drink $18 a week	$936
Tank of Gas	10 gallons at $1.35/gallon per week	$702
Cigarettes	$2 a pack, 2 packs a day, $28/wk	$1456
Six pack of beer	$4 a pack, 2 packs a week, $8/wk	$416
Delivered pizza	$8, one a month	$96
Fast food lunch	$4, 3 per week, $12 per week	$624

		Annual Savings
Clip Coupons	$2 per week	$104
Save	$1 per week	$ 52 plus interest
	$10 per week	$520 plus interest
	$50 per month	$600 plus interest
	$25 per week	$1300 plus interest

INVESTMENT COMPARISON WORKSHEET

Name	Type	Current Price	Term	Future Value	Notes

*S=stock, B=bond, M=mutual fund, R=real estate

NOTES FOR WORKSHEET

ADDITIONAL RESOURCES

When researching, always consider the source of the information to determine any bias that may be hidden in the information given.

Magazines:

>*Money*
>*Kiplinger's Personal Finance Magazine*

Books:

>*The Millionaire Next Door*
>*The Motley Fool Money Guide*
>*The Everything Money Book*

Internet - specific topic, search by whatever you're interested in, except IRA (you'll get the Irish Republican Army).

>**For IRAs go to www.irs.gov**
>**For credit card rates, go to www.bankrate.com**

Internet - good general information sites or calculator sites.

CNNfn.com	**Financenter.com**	**USAToday.com**
Kiplinger.com	**Money.com**	**Myvesta.org**
Fool.com	**truthaboutcredit.org**	**Quicken.com**
Webwinder.com	**TreasuryDirect.gov**	

Helpful software packages:
    Quicken
    TurboTax

You can get free brochures and other *stuff* from most financial institutions.

BIBLIOGRAPHY

College Board, *2002 College Cost and Financial Aid Handbook,* New York, NY, The College Entrance Examination Board, 2002

John Downes and Jordan Elliott Goodman, *Barron's Finance and Investment Handbook,* Woodbury, NY, Barrons, 1986

General Accounting Office, *College Students and Credit Cards,* Washington, D.C., USGAO, June 2001

Jordan Elliott Goodman, *Everyone's Money Book, Second edition,* Chicago IL, Dearborn Financial Publishing, 1998

Richard Mintzer, *The Everything Money Book,* Holbrook MA, Adams Media Corporation, 1999

Jane Bryant Quinn, *Making the Most of Your Money,* New York, Simon and Schuster, 1997

World Book Encyclopedia, 1998

Web Sites:

American Bankruptcy Institute	abiworld.org
Dept. of Education	ed.gov
Federal Reserve	federalreserve.gov
Federal Trade Commission	ftc.gov
General Accounting Office	gao.gov
The Motley Fool	Fool.com
National Association of Colleges and Employers	naceweb.org
Quicken®	quicken.com
U.S. Public Interest Research Group	PIRG.org
	Truthaboutcredit.org
Webwinder	Webwinder.com

Fell's Official Know-It-All Guide™

Check out these exciting titles in our Know-It-All™ series, available at your favorite bookstore:

- ❏ Fell's Official Know-It-All™ Guide: **Advanced Hypnotism**
- ❏ Fell's Official Know-It-All™ Guide: **Advanced Magic**
- ❏ Fell's Official Know-It-All™ Guide: **The Art of Traveling Extravagantly & Nearly**
- ❏ Fell's Official Know-It-All™ Guide: **Budget Weddings**
- ❏ Fell's Official Know-It-All™ Guide: **Career Planning**
- ❏ Fell's Official Know-It-All™ Guide: **Contract Bridge**
- ❏ Fell's Official Know-It-All™ Guide: **Coins 2003**
- ❏ Fell's Official Know-It-All™ Guide: **Cruises**
- ❏ Fell's Official Know-It-All™ Guide: **Defensive Divorce**
- ❏ Fell's Official Know-It-All™ Guide: **Dreams**
- ❏ Fell's Official Know-It-All™ Guide: **Easy Entertaining**
- ❏ Fell's Official Know-It-All™ Guide: **ESP Power**
- ❏ Fell's Official Know-It-All™ Guide: **Getting Rich & Staying Rich**
- ❏ Fell's Official Know-It-All™ Guide: **Health & Wellness**
- ❏ Fell's Official Know-It-All™ Guide: **Hypnotism**
- ❏ Fell's Official Know-It-All™ Guide: **Knots**
- ❏ Fell's Official Know-It-All™ Guide: **Let's Get Results, Not Excuses**
- ❏ Fell's Official Know-It-All™ Guide: **Magic For Beginners**
- ❏ Fell's Official Know-It-All™ Guide: **Mortgage Maze**
- ❏ Fell's Official Know-It-All™ Guide: **No Bull Selling**
- ❏ Fell's Official Know-It-All™ Guide: **Nutrition For a New America**
- ❏ Fell's Official Know-It-All™ Guide: **Online Investing**
- ❏ Fell's Official Know-It-All™ Guide: **Palm Reading**
- ❏ Fell's Official Know-It-All™ Guide: **Relationship Selling**
- ❏ Fell's Official Know-It-All™ Guide: **Secrets of Mind Power**
- ❏ Fell's Official Know-It-All™ Guide: **So, You Want to be a Teacher**
- ❏ Fell's Official Know-It-All™ Guide: **Super Power Memory**
- ❏ Fell's Official Know-It-All™ Guide: **Ultimate Beauty Recipes**
- ❏ Fell's Official Know-It-All™ Guide: **Wedding Planner**
- ❏ Fell's Official Know-It-All™ Guide: **Wisdom in the Office**